Tools
for Team
Excellence

Tools *for* Team Excellence

Getting Your Team Into High Gear and Keeping It There

Gregory E. Huszczo

Davies-Black Publishing

PALO ALTO, CALIFORNIA

Published by Davies-Black Publishing, an imprint of Consulting Psychologists Press, Inc., 3803 East Bayshore Road, Palo Alto, California 94303; 1-800-624-1765.

Special discounts on bulk quantities of Davies-Black books are available to corporations, professional associations, and other organizations. For details, contact the Director of Book Sales at Davies-Black Publishing, 3803 East Bayshore Road, Palo Alto, California 94303; Fax 415-988-0673.

MBTI and *Myers-Briggs Type Indicator* are registered trademarks of Consulting Psychologists Press, Inc.

Cover photograph: Telegraph Colour Lib/FPG International Corp.

99 98 97 96   10 9 8 7 6 5 4 3 2 1

Printed in the United States of America

Library of Congress Cataloging-in-Publication Data
Huszczo, Gregory E.
    Tools for team excellence : getting your team into high gear and keeping it there / Gregory E. Huszczo. — 1st ed.
        p.   cm.
    Includes bibliographical references and index.
    ISBN 0-89106-081-2
    1. Work groups. 2. Performance standards. I. Title.
    HD66.H87 1996
    658.4′02—dc20   95-44374
                                                                              CIP

FIRST EDITION
First printing, 1996

This book is dedicated to my son, Sam...
a great teammate in all aspects of our lives

Contents

List of Exercises

Preface

*"If you don't do it excellently, don't do it at all.
Because if it's not excellent, it won't be profitable
or fun, and if you're not in business for fun or
profit, what the hell are you doing there?"*
—Robert Townsend, *Up the Organization*

Today most companies want to harness the collective power of people working together. All types of organizations are empowering task forces, committees, and teams to come up with the improvements needed to succeed in these times of rapid change. Most companies today emphasize the need for teamwork and for realizing that "we are all in this together." Give me a factory with 350 employees in which the people closest to the action get to provide input on what the problems are and what should be done about them versus a factory where only managers are allowed to think and I will show you a competitive advantage. Most leaders today are convinced that the use of a team approach to running a business has great potential. However, most companies are struggling to come up with a way to help teams be successful. Still other companies are only talking about teams but failing to take the actions necessary to truly encourage team excellence. This book asks the question, What if we took teams seriously? I want you to consider what you and others would be doing differently if teams were the basic building blocks of your organization's structure. What areas need to be worked on in order for your organization to succeed with teams? What are the key ingredients of team excellence?

This book is a no-nonsense, practical guide for establishing, developing, and sustaining excellent teams in your organization. This book will not sell you on the idea of using a team concept. Many other books are available that laud the successes of various team approaches to organizational effectiveness. It assumes that either you or someone with authority in your organization has already decided that teams are the way to go. It assumes that you are either already on a team (as a member or as a leader) or are interested in helping the teams in a given organization get better (as a manager or a member of a human resource staff or as a consultant). As the very successful basketball coach Pat Riley says, "Excellence is the gradual result of always wanting to do better." What you need is a road map and some useful activities to get your teams moving forward. The goal of this book is to provide you with that road map, along with proven exercises and team-training tools to move your teams toward excellence.

The road map presented in this book is the Seven Key Components of Effective Teams, used successfully by teams in organizations for the purpose of improving team performance. Research conducted with more than 100 of the most effective teams in business over the past twenty years has uncovered seven essential components for team excellence—clear sense of direction, talented members, clear and enticing responsibilities, reasonable and efficient operating procedures, constructive interpersonal relationships, active reinforcement systems, and constructive external relationships, both inside and outside the organization. Each of the seven components of team effectiveness is described in detail in this book. Organizations that have benefitted from this model of team excellence include Ford Motor Company, General Motors, Michigan Bell, the University of Michigan, and Navistar International, as well as numerous other manufacturing, service, public, and not-for-profit organizations.

Beyond the use of an understandable and practical road map, the value of this book lies in the structured exercises that will help teams assess and improve themselves within each of the seven components. Each assessment tool and exercise has been used by corporate trainers, organizational consultants, and other professionals, and was specially adapted for use here. Accompanied by instructions for both implementation and follow-up, teams can now use these exercises on their own. Some of the practical applications of the exercises in this book include diagnosing a team's weak spots, developing better relationship and task skills, and solving specific performance problems, as well as learning how to take advantage of a team's key strengths.

Finally, to further enhance the accessible nature of this book, it's written in a down-to-earth, practical tone. It doesn't take a rocket scientist to make teams work. It takes perseverance, integrity, a game plan, and a willingness to learn while doing. Every adult in this society has had some experiences with teams and experience can be a great teacher. Therefore, I know that you already know something about teams. You may have experienced a training seminar on team building. Your company may be in the process of restructuring to establish teams as a business strategy. Even if your current work environment isn't actively experimenting with teams, you certainly have had some experience with groups and teams at some point in your life. What was the best team experience you ever had? Was it a production team? A salaried support staff? A sports team? A choir? Student council? A committee? An emergency evacuation team? A coaching staff? Your current work department? Whatever the nature of the experience, you were probably part of a group that accomplished something and felt good about the people who worked together to reach that goal. You were productive and satisfied.

The best team that I was ever on was an education staff. Although we could have worked very independently, we chose to spend the time and energy needed to benefit from interacting and depending on each other. We held regular staff meetings that reminded us what it was that we were attempting to collectively accomplish. We informed each other of our plans, our successes, and our frustrations. Teammates supported each other but also made it clear that we expected no less than 100 percent effort from any member of the staff. Colleagues challenged staff members to keep the information and teaching techniques fresh and engaging. We sought information from the "students" (full-time employees and/or leaders in the organization) who attended our sessions to find out not only whether they enjoyed their interactions with us but also whether they actually used what we "taught." Everyone on this team knew the role she or he was expected to play to make this staff successful. We solved problems together and dedicated little time to figuring out who was to blame. We knew we would all be better off focusing on what the issues were rather than on who deserved credit or blame. That doesn't mean we didn't express appreciation to members who behaved in a team-oriented manner. Individuals who did things—ordinary things as well as extraordinary things—that helped our staff get its work done were made aware of it. We even made sure that people in the larger organization for whom we worked received credit when they provided us with resources or information, or even when they just followed through on their promises. We had an appointed leader who went to bat for us, encouraged us to provide input on decisions beyond our own tasks and assignments, and wasn't threatened by the fact that team members knew more about many things than she did. We weren't perfect, but we dealt with our imperfections. We got the job done well and all had very satisfying work experiences. I have been fortunate to be on some other effective teams, but most of my time has been spent consulting for organizations in the process of developing their own teams.

I have spent my entire adult life studying and working with teams. I have learned about teams as a researcher, a change agent, a teacher, and a team member. As a kid, I was fascinated by sports teams. I became curious as to why some teams seemed to have so much talent yet failed to succeed. Personally, I also experienced some teams in which members got along well with each other but didn't really succeed on the playing field. Team success didn't seem to be merely a matter of talent *or* good relations. I thought maybe it was a matter of having a good coach. But different coaching styles also failed to explain success rates.

My curiosity about teams led me to go to college to become a math teacher and basketball coach. I also started taking some psychology courses and found the descriptions of group dynamics fascinating. Later, I became part of a work team. We were the resanding team of the paint department in a Big Three truck plant. If there was a sag in the paint job or if some dust fell on the truck as it went through the oven after it was painted, it would be rerouted to a spur on the assembly line where our team would surround it and sand it down with pneumatic and hand sanders. I enjoyed being part of a team rather than reading about them. However, I became increasingly frustrated by how our team's ideas were ignored by the company. To make a long story short, I got fired or threatened every time we tried to make a difference. School started to look better to me after these experiences.

I later returned to school to study industrial and organizational psychology, but my days in that truck plant changed my life. I have studied, researched, and consulted for organizational change efforts that utilize employee involvement strategies through the use of teams for more than twenty years now. I have worked with over 100 companies, primarily in unionized settings. Throughout this book, I will share what I have learned from my experiences and from my own and others' research on the use of teams. I have seen both good and bad examples of the application of the team concept. Unfortunately, I have seen more examples of organizations talking about implementing teams than I have seen genuine efforts to empower teams as an effective business strategy. When I am asked to help an organization with its efforts to institute a team approach, I have to sort out just what is really behind the request. Sometimes I find out that some executive went to a seminar or read a book and decided it would be great to join the movement toward teams. Others seem to see teams as a means of reducing employees. Many confuse team building with teamwork. By that, I mean that they want people to cooperate (be team players) and go along with a plan that has already been decided.

However, some companies genuinely want to take teams seriously. Key leaders believe that groups of knowledgeable and skilled employees can make better decisions than the average individual. They see teams as a vehicle for people to relate to the organization that they work for. They see teams as the key structure for gaining commitment. They want the teams to work effectively and efficiently, providing high-quality goods and/or services to accomplish the goals of the organization. They recognize that teams cannot operate in a vacuum and that they need support and resources. Some leaders want a system that provides a disciplined but humane approach for organizing work through teams.

The main purpose of this book is to share with you the system that I have seen make a difference. If you and your organization want to build team excellence, you need to prepare the grounds to nurture team development. The chapters in part 1 of this book explain the basic framework for understanding teams, diagnosing current levels of effectiveness, and getting started with team-building sessions. Exercises will help you assess a team and the strategies to prepare the organization and the team members for success.

The chapters of part 2 contain the Seven Key Components of Effective Teams that my research and experience indicate are needed for building team effectiveness—a clear sense of direction, talented members, clear and enticing responsibilities, reasonable and efficient operating procedures, constructive interpersonal relationships, active reinforcement systems, and constructive external relationships. These chapters will also provide you with numerous tools, techniques, and exercises to help your teams improve on each of these dimensions. These tools and exercises are presented in a way that enables any team member to use them. They are not motivational speeches or "touchy–feely" activities aimed at inspiring people to believe in teams. They just make sense if you want your team to become better than it is today. This section of the book will provide down-to-earth help in attaining team excellence. After all, the purpose of team building in organizations is not to produce teams, it is to help teams produce for the organization and become more satisfying experiences for team members.

The final part of this book emphasizes the need to view team development as a process, not a program. Strategies are needed to sustain the successful use of a team approach. No team is ever perfect. There is always room for improvement. It is my hope that this book will provide you with insights regarding your current situation and the practical tools needed to enhance the effectiveness and satisfaction levels of your organization's teams. Your actual approach to helping teams will vary, depending on the politics and history of the situation. The procedures and strategies that should be used must vary, depending on whether you are attempting to help a task force, a committee, a traditional work unit, or a self-directed work team. While the depth of the intervention may vary, I have found the seven-component model to still provide the road map needed to plan for, or return to, the journey toward continuous improvement. Please let me know what elements you find most useful and share with me techniques you have discovered that will enhance any of the seven components. You can send your feedback and experiences to me in care of the publisher.

Acknowledgments

Public thanks are in order for the many people who have provided me with the experiences that led to the writing of this book. I am especially grateful to the hundreds of team members in the organizations that I have consulted for. They educated me on what helped and what hindered their work lives. They allowed me to listen and learn from them. I also want to thank my son, Sam, for understanding that it was important for me to spend the time needed to write this book. He made the time that I wasn't writing so enjoyable and helped me keep a balance in my life. I also want to thank my parents, Edward and Virginia, who always encouraged me to learn and to work. They helped develop in me a belief in myself and a way to value education and work experience. I want to thank my colleagues and students in our master's program in human resources and organizational development. They helped critique my ideas about teams and stimulated me to improve my early models. I want to thank my teammates in the world of sports and in the world of work. Without them, I would not have had any direct experiences to draw from. Many people have contributed to my own education but a few key "mentors" helped mold my thinking about the concepts relevant to this book. Dr. Carl Frost instilled in me the importance of being a client-centered process consultant. He taught me the value of asking questions, not merely offering answers. Dr. Cecil Williams introduced me to the *Myers-Briggs Type Indicator®* (MBTI®). This has helped me value individual differences in a very practical and meaningful way. Don Ephlin and Irving Bluestone, former vice presidents of the United Auto Workers, taught me a lot about leadership and risk taking. Their actions showed me what can happen when you take teams seriously. Finally, I want to thank the people who have encouraged me to write this book, such as Sandra Hirsh and the people at Consulting Psychologists Press and Davies-Black Publishing, especially Lee Langhammer Law, Melinda Adams Merino, and Allen Hammer, for all the support and helpful ideas throughout the writing and preparation of this book.

PART ONE

Preparing for Team Excellence

T he chapters in this section of the book will help you understand the variety of team types that are used in organizations today, how you can prepare your company for the advent of teams, and how you can help prepare the people who will be on these teams. Developing effective teams is not unlike growing a garden. If you want to grow a great garden, you don't just buy expensive seeds and throw them into any plot of soil. You choose a plot of land that will receive adequate sunlight. You rototill the earth. You space the seeds according to the types of plants you want to grow. You provide plenty of water, and remove the weeds that will choke production. If your organization is serious about developing productive teams—committees, task forces, departments, or self-directed work teams that produce a high-quality product or satisfy customers with desired services—many people in the organization are going to have to follow the example of successful gardeners.

Chapter 1 provides the basic information regarding the variety of teams you might want to establish, and the potential benefits of using teams for both the people on them and the organization. The seven key ingredients teams need to prosper will also be introduced. Chapter 2 explains how to prepare the garden plot in which the teams are to grow. Five steps must be taken in order for teams to be used as a business strategy. Support mechanisms such as steering committees and design teams must research the need for teams and sketch the blueprint for the types of teams that are to be grown and the timetable and rules for caring for such teams. Leaders inside and outside of these teams must use a style that is conducive to nurturing and harvesting these teams. Most important, if the organization is going to be serious about growing excellent teams, actions must follow the words and plans that are presented. Chapter 3 outlines the basic nuts and bolts of preparing the people, or seeds, themselves. Questions to be addressed include: How do you pick people to be on committees and task forces and self-directed work teams? What input should be sought from team members to help launch or enhance teams? What are the various methods that can be used to assess your teams and gain this input? What kind of training should be provided to team members? What mistakes are commonly made in how this team training is provided? Chapter 3 answers these questions and provides tools and examples that will help you determine what is needed to get your garden of teams in good shape. Before we begin, let's take a look at a real-life example of how one organization moved toward a team concept approach as its key business strategy to maintain its number one status in its industry.

Case Study

A Request for Teams in a Service Organization

The director of training and development of the Finance and Controllers Division of a large service organization that employs financial analysts, business planners, computer programmers, systems developers, accountants, lawyers, and technicians (all of whom are salaried professionals and/or managers) was asked by the key manager in the Financial Analysis Department, "What can be done to establish a team approach to the work of this division?" This key manager had become interested in the "team concept" through articles he read in newspapers and magazines. He also noticed that the corporation that the division belonged to had begun using the term *team* in its advertisements. He thought it would be astute to demonstrate some leadership on this team issue, which he happened to like as a concept anyway.

The company decided to send out a survey to the division's 400 employees, which contained two questions: "Do you support a team approach to doing things?" and "Would you like some team training?" Everyone responded yes to the first question and most (350) responded that they would like to receive some team training. Now the organization needed to find something that would fulfill this seemingly widespread need.

The director of training and development received a flyer about a one-day program offered by a well-known consulting firm. He, the key manager of finance, and one associate attended the session. The three returned from the program enthused about teams but unsure about how they could make things happen within their organization. They also noticed that once they were back at work, their feelings about the seminar faded and they didn't feel any better prepared to deal with their colleagues on the day-to-day realities of getting work done.

Should they just send more representatives to these seminars whenever scheduling permitted? That would be a convenient and relatively inexpensive way of following through on the requests of employees for team training. They decided instead to form a Training Advisory Council and charge it with the responsibility of identifying three alternative means of providing team training and, ultimately, developing a plan for establishing a team approach within every department in the Finance and Controllers Division. The council consisted of ten people from a variety of departments and represented four of the five levels of management that existed in the division. The council was to report directly to the director of training and development, who then was to make a final recommendation to the general manager of the division.

At the first meeting of the council, the members listened politely as the key manager and the director of training and development explained their division's interest in establishing a team approach and the level of interest expressed by employees on the survey. Finally, one member made it clear that he meant no offense but needed reassurance that this effort was going to be for real. He pointed out how the corporation had launched a quality circles effort a few years ago. Two years later, they set up what they called Quality of Work Life Teams. Then all of their employees attended Total Quality Management training. He wanted to know how this council was going to convince people that this interest in teams was serious. Other members then pointed out that they felt certain departments in the division already operated as effective teams. The meeting ended with commitments from the manager of financial analysis to discuss the issues with the general manager of the division; from the director of training and development to identify no fewer than three providers of organizational development consulting and team training services; and from several members to talk with people from team-oriented departments to discover the "secrets" of successful teams.

All of these commitments were fulfilled. In fact, over the next several meetings, it became standard for the group to begin each meeting checking whether people had kept their commitments and ending each meeting with statements regarding what new commitments were being made. Council members began to trust each other and the organization itself. This "team" to plan for teams got enthused about making this effort to bring about organizational change a genuine and long-lasting one. They listened to presentations from four consultants. Two offered set programs emphasizing the importance of having a good attitude and getting along with others. They were politely but quickly shown the door. The council picked a consultant who asked questions during his presentation rather than declaring what the division really needed. He suggested that the survey on teams previously administered was probably not valid. He proposed that he would conduct a series of confidential interviews with a sample of about thirty-five to forty members of the division that would represent the organization, both horizontally and vertically. He would then try to determine whether people actually saw a need for moving toward a team approach to performing the work of the division; what people thought their departments already did well; what they envisioned things would be like if this "team concept" really succeeded over the next three years; what would help the division successfully become team oriented and what might interfere with that goal. He thought the results should be analyzed by the council before any team training sessions took place and that the sessions should be tailored differently for each team that volunteered to go through the training. He presented a model of what he suspected were the key ingredients of successful teams and negotiated an agreement that included a requirement that each team fill out a questionnaire based on his model at least once a year over the next three years.

So instead of taking the convenient path of sending division members to the exciting one-day seminar on teams, no training was offered for four months. During that time, interviews were conducted; the results were analyzed and shared with the entire division; the general manager made a clear statement of the range of decisions that teams could make under the "team concept approach"; team leaders were asked to help design the training that best suited their teams' needs; and team data were gathered on a regular basis and provided to all team members. Team training sessions were offered on an ongoing basis. The sessions themselves weren't so much training as they were focused discussions about how members were going to improve their efforts to get tasks done and how relationships were to be improved. Each team was expected to develop a one-year plan for team excellence. Every year, each team was to present an annual report of its progress and its next "Team Excellence Strategic Plan" to the general manager and to the Training Advisory Council.

The results were far from perfect but clearly recognizable. Errors in billing procedures became almost nonexistent; software development efforts were expedited and provided throughout the corporation in a manner that minimized the need for detailed explanations; financial analysis reports were written in an understandable way; levels of morale as measured on the yearly survey improved; and every team had a clear list of the things it needed to do to become more effective.

Not all teams reported success. The dramatic changes in the industry required many changes in membership of the teams within the division. It seemed just when interpersonal relationships improved on a given team, people changed jobs. However, the division gained the reputation for being the corporate leaders in making the team concept successful. Members of the Training Advisory Council were frequently asked to make presentations to groups throughout the company. Some received promotions to corporate-level positions. The director of training and development retired, and his replacement had little experience with team approaches and preferred an emphasis on technical training programs offered to all members.

The system for continually improving team effectiveness survived these changes. It became part of the way business was conducted in the division. The efforts made by the original leaders in the division to prepare the organization and its members for a team concept paid off. The next three chapters are designed to help you think through the issues that you and others within your organization should consider before launching any efforts to make teams effective and satisfying.

CHAPTER 1

The Nature of Teams in Organizations

Although the United States is generally thought of as a culture that emphasizes individualism, teams can be found everywhere. Businesses are particularly interested in teams nowadays. Nearly every Fortune 500 company reports having some form of an employee involvement process in place. Forming teams is a natural way to involve employees in an organization, especially in larger organizations. Problem-solving committees, quality improvement groups, task forces, product launch teams, quality circles, and self-directed work teams are key elements of strategies that recognize that every employee in an organization has expertise that can contribute to the success of the enterprise. This actually represents a major shift in management thinking.

Moving Past Taylor's Model

The classical school of thought, characterized by F. W. Taylor's (1911) *Scientific Management,* is finally being viewed as a detriment to the continued success of American business organizations. Taylor suggested that workers are "as dumb as oxen" and that management must provide all the brainpower in an organization. He thought that managers should systematically (i.e., scientifically) analyze each job and identify the one best way to get the job done. In Taylor's mind, the workers should then be told exactly how to do the work, and if they complied, they should be rewarded. If labor unrest rears its ugly head, this approach suggests that all that needs to be done is to dangle a little more money to motivate workers to use the system designed by management. This approach actually had its share of successes in the first half of the twentieth century. Production efficiency was the chief concern. Quality and innovation were of lesser importance. Threats from international competition were minimal, and the attitude of Don't question authority! prevailed.

But things are different today. In fact, the whole rate of change itself has changed. Companies today that are not flexible do not stay in business. Information flows rapidly all over the world. Customers demand quality, and competition is fierce. Employees at all levels are more knowledgeable than in previous times and are more comfortable challenging authority. Companies today must benefit from the input that their employees can provide and gain the commitment, not just the compliance, of their workers. Organizational change is not easy, and many times, efforts to change are not successful. Teams provide the underlying structure for most organizational development efforts. The knowledge and skills needed to build excellent teams are crucial for anyone willing to help an organization become effective and satisfying.

What's in a Team?

The main structure available to "harvest" the input and provide the sense of meaningful involvement in an organization is the team. However, what a team means in one organization may differ dramatically from what it means in another. The most generic definition of a team emphasizes that it is two or more people interacting together to accomplish a common purpose. Later in this chapter, we will investigate what it takes to have an effective team. For our purposes here, the many potential benefits of teams include:

- Providing an important source of stimulation
- Creating higher-quality solutions than most individuals working alone can create
- Providing structure that encourages a sense of involvement in a large organization
- Serving as a vehicle for organizational development efforts
- Offering a means of satisfying relationship/belongingness needs and thus providing a source of satisfaction
- Providing a forum for constructive conflict resolution

- Providing an opportunity for more individuals to develop and utilize leadership skills and fulfill personal needs
- Improving productivity through a more flexible approach to utilizing the knowledge and skills of employees
- Bringing about a structure that helps employees address the fact that everyone needs to depend on each other in order for the organization to succeed

In 1975, Harold J. Leavitt pointed out that fifty years of research established the powerful effect of small groups of employees on productivity and satisfaction levels in business organizations. He wondered, what would be different "if we really used groups, rather than individuals as the basic building blocks for an organization." Over the last two decades, company after company has declared its interest in the "team concept." Yet there seems to be much more talk than action on this front. Too often, managers say they are interested in teams, but they seem to confuse the notions of teamwork—that is, cooperation—with team building. This book will help organizations sort out the motivations for teams and propose systematic approaches that will enable them to take teams seriously.

The Five Major Team Types

There are five main types of teams found in organizations. Table 1 outlines the main team types and illustrates some of their defining characteristics. This book will focus on strategies to improve the effectiveness and satisfaction levels of most of these types. It will not treat the informal sense of a team, or the "We are all in this together" approach to the team concept, as a serious effort at team building.

An Informal Sense of Teams

Some organizations want to emphasize that employees across every department and every level need to realize that they are all in this together. Top management wants togetherness, cooperation—"one big happy family." The notion here is to think of the whole company as a team that is competing against other companies. Management may share more information with the workforce. It may put up motivational posters and hold pep rallies to encourage employees to feel

Table 1 The Five Major Team Types

1. Informal sense of a team
   "We are all in this together"
   The whole company

2. Traditional work units with a supervisor
   Departments
   Sections
   Staff
   Office
   Those that don't require much interaction/interdependency
   Those that do require much interaction/interdependency

3. Problem-solving task forces, committees, and circles
   Temporary cross-functional teams
   Skip level teams
   Problem-solving teams (project centered, work centered)
   Quality circles

4. Leadership teams, steering committees, and advisory councils
   Leadership teams
   Steering committees
   Councils
   Advisory teams

5. Self-directed work teams
   Self-regulating work groups
   Team concept
   Semiautonomous work groups
   Cell management
   Area supervision
   Small business units

what is good for the company will be good for them. While there is nothing inherently wrong with this notion, the lack of structures encouraging two-way interaction leaves little room for employee input. It does appear that some companies use this approach to gain compliance to plans already established by upper management. This approach to a team concept often lacks substance and feels like brain-washing to many employees. At its best, this approach is a motivational and inspirational means of tapping employee loyalty. At its worst, it is paternalism or exploitation.

Traditional Work Units

Virtually all businesses are organized into groups of employees. The groupings are called many different things, such as departments, sections, and units, and members are expected to accomplish a function, produce a product, or provide a service, or at least all report to the same person in the chain of command, such as a supervisor or manager. If the work is so independent that the members do not need to interact at all to accomplish their assignments, then we might not want to call this group a team at all. The greater the need to interact and the more dependent each member is on the other members' efforts to do their own jobs, the more the group truly resembles a team. Managers of these traditional work units might reinforce this sense of "teamness" by facilitating interaction between members by holding meetings or establishing expectations that hold two or more members jointly responsible for aspects of the work to be accomplished. Some managers have held assumptions about workers that are quite different from Taylor's *Scientific Management* model. Some emphasized working as teams long before the concept became popular. Some emphasized a team approach when times were good, only to revert to autocratic control under crisis conditions. Some thought that it would be better for the employees who reported to them to get along with each other without realizing that to function as a team, you need to be task and relationship oriented.

Problem-Solving Task Forces, Committees, and Circles

Some companies allow subgroups to meet periodically to investigate problems and then either make recommendations or actually resolve the problems. In fact, this has been a path many companies have taken in their first efforts to tap the power of teams. The successful use of quality circles over the last forty years to turn around Japan's manufacturing organizations has been well documented. In a *quality circle,* a group of employees volunteer to systematically study a work process and recommend ways to improve the quality of the process and the product. They typically meet for one hour a week and apply statistical process control techniques to research the problem while learning to work effectively together.

While American companies have used white-collar task forces and committees for decades, allowing blue-collar employees to voluntarily join circles, task forces, and committees was resisted for the most part until the 1980s. The term quality circles has often been avoided in the United States. The basics of circles, however, have existed under the auspices of the "quality of work life," "employee involvement," and the Total Quality Management movements over the last two decades. The range of problems that can be addressed and the actual decision-making power of these teams differ dramatically from company to company. Generally the term *task force* infers that the team is formed to investigate a particular problem and is then dissolved once it identifies recommendations to solve the problem. Problem-solving teams and committees usually have the charter to continually identify problems and perhaps bring in outside resources if the committee members do not have the expertise to deal with a specific issue. Problem-solving teams, committees, and task forces typically report to a steering committee or to the level of management needed to resolve the problem. They do not typically have the authority to take the necessary actions to resolve the problem themselves.

Most attempts at team building that have problem-solving groups as their key component follow a pattern of: (1) expending considerable effort to reduce fears and provide training in group dynamics and problem solving to volunteers, (2) having some successful pilot teams that make things more comfortable for employees and/or solve some productivity and quality issues, (3) expanding the number of teams that, in turn, produces a challenge for production scheduling and some signs of burnout, and (4) having interest in this approach to teams either fading away or expanding the power of teams to make their own decisions and perhaps even run their area of the business. Less than 30 percent of efforts to establish employee involvement/quality of work life/problem-solving teams last for more than five years. Strategies for sustaining the successful use of teams will be discussed in chapter 11.

Leadership Teams, Steering Committees, and Advisory Councils

Steering committees and other top-level leadership teams represent an interesting attempt to establish team concepts in American companies. They can be the most difficult teams to develop since they are often composed of individuals who are used to being in charge of their own portions of the organization. In unionized companies, they are typically composed of the top union leaders and the key managers of a particular location. This has led to some dramatic improvements in labor relations at some locations, where grievance rates have plummeted, jobs have been saved, and quality has been improved. Union and management have sometimes united in their mutual interest to keep customers satisfied. At their best, steering committees have provided a model for the rest of the organization of how employees can work together on a team and the power and support that are needed for other teams to succeed in the company.

However, this has also led to considerable controversy. Factions within some unions have accused leaders of "cozying up with management." Some middle- and lower-level managers have complained about feeling that the "union is now running the plant" or that management is playing favorites through its selection of who is on the steering committee in non-union plants.

Leadership teams in nonunion environments are important to establish because middle-level managers in particular often feel left out and threatened by team concept efforts. Some companies form a management council and have this team participate in strategic planning. Others establish separate teams of middle-level and supervisory-level managers and ask them to address as a team issues that cut across departmental lines. These teams can also be difficult to build effectively. The members may be used to being the person-in-charge in their own departments and have difficulty working with peers. Organizational politics and strong egos may create obstacles to team effectiveness. This book will provide a roadmap and the tools to deal with these problems.

Self-Directed Work Teams

The team concept that has received the most attention in the 1990s is the movement toward self-directed work teams (SDWT), also known as self-regulating work teams, semiautonomous work groups, and leaderless teams. Wellins, Byham, and Wilson (1991) define an SDWT as "an intact group of employees who are responsible for a whole work process or segment that delivers a product or service to an internal or external customer" (p. 3). However, they also point out that there is no such thing as a typical team. Although their research indicates that these teams do not exist in the majority of companies, 78 percent of their large sample of organizations believes they will have SDWTs by the year 2000.

Although the title SDWT implies that no manager or supervisor is part of these teams, in practice, they sometimes are. In fact, the variations in SDWTs are quite great, perhaps in part because it is so popular to say a company has such an innovation. Sometimes the title of the manager within such a team is changed to coach or facilitator. Sometimes the manager is given several teams to oversee and she or he is given the title of area manager. Perhaps most commonly, the team is asked to elect an hourly employee to serve as a team coordinator. Occasionally, the team is asked to distribute all of the leadership responsibilities equally across its membership.

Although there is no one format that can describe how an SDWT should operate, research from several sources addressing this topic suggests that ideally SDWTs need to:

- Be collectively responsible for an identifiable piece of the company's business
- Have clear, measurable daily evidence with which they can verify whether they are succeeding
- Have members with varying skills, abilities, and problem-solving strategies
- Have little or no status differences among members
- Have opportunities for members to interact and meet easily/ frequently
- Be structured to have interdependent job responsibilities
- Engage in cross-training or at least cross-education on all of the jobs on the team
- Have the authority to make decisions about how to get the work done
- Be given a mixture of individual and group rewards
- Be provided frequent offers of assistance and encouragement from external coaches and resource people

It is difficult for a team with more than ten members to manage itself. The power and authority of the team tend to expand across time and as the training needed to take on more responsibilities is provided. Team members generally have the right to decide how to get the job done, who gets assigned to which jobs, and they may have some input regarding production level expectations. They must maintain quality standards and are expected to interact directly with their "customers" and "suppliers" to ensure satisfaction. As members move on to other assignments, SDWTs often select member replacements themselves.

They may also be given the responsibility to evaluate performance, take disciplinary actions, and even remove group members. However, this is not typical and is clearly something that would not be well received in most unionized environments. In fact, many elements of common variations of SDWTs may violate clauses in union contracts regarding such things as job classifications and wage rates for group leaders and the principles of solidarity. However, SDWTs appear frequently in unionized firms. Separate Letters of Agreement, often referred to as Modern Operating Agreements, need to be negotiated. It is probably best to put agreements regarding SDWTs in writing in nonunion firms as well. Much planning and preparation must take place to successfully implement the SDWT form of the team concept. The steps and procedures to prepare an organization and the team members themselves will be discussed in chapter 2.

Although there are many pitfalls to deal with in SDWTs, including frustration, resistance to change, some employees taking advantage of their power, and reduction in employment levels, research indicates that such teams consistently outperform traditionally designed work groups (Pearce and Ravlin, 1987). Increased productivity as well as improvements in employee satisfaction and reduced absenteeism, turnover, and accident rates have been documented. There is even more evidence for improvements in attitudes and process changes than those made in productivity, but virtually no evidence suggests that decreases in productivity occur for firms that get through the early phases of SDWTs. These gains do not come automatically. SDWTs need continual care. This approach to teams, or any approach that makes a serious attempt to establish teams in an organization, for that matter, requires a process, not a program. My seven-component model, which I'll address next, provides such a process.

The Seven Key Components of Effective Teams

Teams should be thought of as human organisms that must be fed, nurtured, and taught. However, you do not need to send your team to a professional team doctor for an annual physical. You can examine any team yourself. Your checkup requires information from the "patient" itself on seven key dimensions. The chart on page 16 contains the

The Seven Key Components of Effective Teams

1. Clear sense of direction

    Shared purpose

    Goals and values understood and perceived as appropriate

2. Talented members

    Full complement of competencies/knowledge/skills available that are relevant to the tasks at hand

    Talents are utilized and developed further

3. Clear and enticing responsibilities

    Expectations of leadership and other roles are well established

    Players understand how their roles fit in the game plan

4. Reasonable and efficient operating procedures

    Task content and process systems are in place to plan, conduct meetings, identify and solve problems, make decisions, give and receive information, evaluate progress, and perform tasks

5. Constructive interpersonal relationships

    Group maintenance systems to celebrate diversity, handle conflict, provide support and challenge

6. Active reinforcement systems

    Desired rewards and accountability for group and individuals

7. Constructive external relationships

    Good diplomatic relations with other groups, people, and subsystems

    Pursue opportunities

    Address threats

Seven Key Components of Effective Teams, the model that serves as a framework for this book. It is based on research and the experience of over 100 teams from a wide variety of organizational settings. These teams completed a diagnostic instrument that is provided for your use in chapter 3. These teams used the model to design their efforts to improve themselves. Exercises to help your teams help themselves on each of these components are provided in chapters 4 through 10. This model will provide you with a road map for team excellence, serving as a repair manual of sorts for assembling and maintaining the teams you want to help.

1. Clear Sense of Direction

Upper management is responsible for setting a company's direction. Moving toward a team concept does not mean that it is time to abdicate that responsibility. An empowered team does not get to do whatever it pleases. The team is empowered to figure out *how* to accomplish what needs to be accomplished. The purpose of each team must be clearly stated. The members of each team must perceive the purpose statement, that is, its charter, to be appropriate. Teams should not exist for the sake of being teams. Teams must have goals and targets to accomplish. Chapter 4 will examine this component and the strategies that could help your team establish clear goals that members will be committed to.

2. Talented Members

The full range of knowledge and skills needed to accomplish set goals must exist on the team or be readily available to the team. The talent not only needs to exist; it must also be utilized. Many teams fail to inventory the talent that exists among their members. Team members may also fail to continually develop their knowledge and skills. They may need to learn the jobs of their teammates and the skills associated with utilizing systematic problem solving and effective meetings. Each member must take responsibility for updating his or her knowledge and skill levels to keep up with the rapid pace of change in today's society. Organizations must utilize selection procedures and provide training and education opportunities to ensure that this component is fulfilled. Chapter 5 will discuss the talent component of effective teams in depth.

3. Clear and Enticing Responsibilities

Each member must know the role she or he is to play in order for the team to succeed. Team members are to fulfill task roles and the relationship-building roles needed to work together. Team members must be able to depend on their teammates to fulfill these responsibilities. This may be one reason why many individuals initially resist efforts to establish a team concept. If an organization is taking the team approach seriously, it must dedicate the time to facilitate the clarification of roles. The role of the leader must also be clarified. The expectations regarding how the functions of leadership will be fulfilled on self-directed work teams is a particularly important factor. Chapter 6 will discuss a variety of strategies for clarifying team roles and responsibilities.

4. Reasonable and Efficient Operating Procedures

Professional sports teams have clearly defined plays and procedures for succeeding. They differ from playground teams, where individuals operate in a freewheeling manner. This book will emphasize the importance of using a disciplined but not overly rigid approach to getting things done. Team members must understand the steps involved in producing their product or providing their service. When these work procedures are followed, team members are more likely to feel comfortable about depending on each other. That is the essence of trust. In addition, teams need procedures to solve problems, conduct meetings, make decisions, generate plans, give and receive information, and evaluate their progress. Chapter 7 will provide a process for teams interested in improving on this component.

5. Constructive Interpersonal Relationships

Team members do not need to be best friends to be a part of a great team. However, team members must demonstrate genuine respect to each other. Since teams made up of members from various backgrounds and of various skills outproduce teams of homogenous composition, teams must celebrate diversity in order to fulfill this component. It helps to understand the differing personalities on the team and see the strengths in those differences. Chapter 8 will provide an explanation of how the *Myers-Briggs Type Indicator* (MBTI) personality framework can help team members understand each other's personalities and use strategies for resolving conflict effectively.

6. Active Reinforcement Systems

Members must feel that their efforts to work in a team-oriented fashion are appreciated. Organizations must seriously look at their evaluation and reward systems to determine if they are reinforcing the behaviors that they claim to want. Team members themselves must free up their willingness to express appreciation to each other as well. If you take behaviors for granted and fail to recognize when expectations are fulfilled, these behaviors may be extinguished. Chapter 9 will examine options for activating this component, which is so often missing in efforts to establish teams in organizational settings today.

7. Constructive External Relationships

Teams not only have to get their own act together, they must also build diplomatic ties with key players and other teams external to their own membership. Teams need to coordinate things with their "suppliers" and satisfy their "customers." Teams need help from resource people, like those in purchasing, maintenance, and human resources. Team members would be smart to have clear communications with managers and union leaders who may not have direct contact on a daily basis but certainly can influence the sense of direction that will affect the operations of teams throughout the organization. In particular, team members must feel that once decisions are made, their teammates won't bad-mouth the team to other people within the organization. Chapter 10 will discuss strategies for teams to develop more constructive external relationships.

Summary

Teams are made up of two or more people working together to accomplish something and, while businesses have utilized teams as a basic organizing principle for decades, the emphasis on teams has been particularly evident over the last twenty years. Despite all the talk, many organizations have failed to reap the benefits of a team approach because they have failed to systematically take the necessary steps to make teams effective. Some organizations did not really want teams; they only wanted compliant and cooperative employees. Some managers attempted to launch team concepts in their organizations because it sounded like the in thing to do. For them, it was a fad. Some managers just wanted to make their employees happy and launched team efforts that encouraged fun and camaraderie. This book is aimed at people in organizations who want to take teams seriously. Teams provide a vehicle for improvements in job satisfaction *and* organizational effectiveness. The remaining chapters of this book will provide a set of processes to assess teams, prepare your organization and systematically develop the effectiveness of teams, and sustain the successes your teams will bring you. The concepts and values underlying team concept can be portrayed as sacred as motherhood and apple pie. The work required to establish genuine, operational, successful teams is not for the fainthearted. It will require some soul searching regarding the motives behind establishing teams. It will try one's patience and one's willingness to trust others. It will take time and resources. This book will not help you develop a freewheeling playground pickup team, but it will help you develop the plans and provide the tools needed to develop a disciplined team approach to becoming the championship team in your industry.

CHAPTER 2

Preparing Organizations for Teams

To establish effective teams in your organization, you will need to prepare the organization, its systems, and its people for the change effort. A key difference between operating a business in the first half of this century and the second half is that businesses today must deal with a faster rate of change. Information flows faster than it ever has before. There is significantly more global competition. Customers demand quality and feel that if it isn't delivered, they can find someone else who will deliver it. The age of the stable organization is over. Virtually every organization has attempted all kinds of changes to cope with these phenomena. Companies are downsizing, reengineering, attempting to become learning organizations, and instituting total quality processes. Many attempts at organizational change fail. If you have ever attempted to lose weight, quit smoking, or take on a more positive view of life, you know that change can be difficult, even for an individual to undertake. Changing the many people and systems associated with an organization, especially one that has had a long history, is clearly much more difficult.

The Five Key Steps to Successful Organizational Change

Why is it that some organizations successfully produce the changes needed to transform themselves and others merely talk about it? Since it is so crucial for organizations to manage change, we need to know about the key steps that lead to success. Establishing effective teams must be thought of as an organizational change effort. The five key steps, outlined in table 2 and detailed throughout this chapter, must initially be put into place.

Becoming Aware of the Need for Change

Organizations don't change simply because someone came up with a good idea. Organizations consider change when enough pain is felt as a result of current practices or when a golden opportunity presents itself. Some key opinion leaders in the organization must conclude that things can't just go on the way they always have. They talk to enough people and, if there is sufficient dissatisfaction with the status quo, change is then considered. There must be a realization that an emphasis on individualism does not serve the organization or its people. There must be a compelling reason to consider establishing a team-oriented structure. Unless at least 80 percent of the members of the organization see a need for change, it will be difficult for a long-term successful change to occur. That does not mean that 80 percent of the organization must support a team concept. It just means that to begin such a process, at least 80 percent of the people need to be unhappy enough with the current situation to want some kind of change.

The awareness stage usually begins with one or two key nonapathetic people searching for a better way of doing things. Maybe someone—ideally, a key opinion leader—reads a book or magazine article or attends a seminar or conference on teams. This person should be thought of as a catalyst for discussion on the need for change, not necessarily on the team concept per se. At this point in the process this catalyst must face a dilemma. Care should be exercised to avoid moving too fast and raising expectations unrealistically, but input from others is needed. Others need to be included in this discussion early on because you want to avoid having the organization think of teams as some individual's idea. It shouldn't be assumed that teams are the answer to the problem, since the problems haven't been defined yet. Ownership by a broad range of employees throughout an organization is one of the key points of any successful change effort. It is much more likely that a broad segment of an organization will reach a consensus decision that change is needed rather than agreement as to which particular approach to change is more desirable.

Table 2 The Five Key Steps to Successful Organizational Change

1. **Becoming aware of the need for change**

   Scanning the environment

   Assessing the current situation

   Recognizing the current problems

   Anticipating the potential opportunities and threats

   Unfreezing the status quo

   Communicating the need for change

2. **Developing a vision of what could and should be**

   Picturing the direction the organization should be headed

   Declaring the values that the organization stands for

   Identifying the strategic options to consider

   Identifying how the organization will know if it is succeeding

3. **Drafting a plan to move the organization toward its vision**

   Identifying the steps that will take it forward

   Organizing a structure that will facilitate the changes

   Soliciting input on the plan and utilizing it

   Clarifying a time frame for actions

   Identifying the resources needed for the changes

4. **Providing the leadership and support for the changes**

   Having key players lead the change with words and actions

   Having champions of the cause take some initiatives and risks

   Sharing the responsibility for leadership

   Clarifying opportunities to participate in the change

   Providing the training needed for employees to participate

   Allowing the time needed to work on the change effort

   Providing the resources needed to work on the change

   Having a few friends in the right places

   Having some luck (e.g., no marketplace disasters)

   Providing recognition for those participating in the change

5. **Following through on the change plan**

   Taking actions consistent with the words of the vision

   Encouraging experimentation

   Implementing the recommendations to solve the problems

   Evaluating the impact of the change efforts

   Revising the change strategies and plans thoughtfully

Forming a Steering Committee

In order to establish the need for change, upper management should form a Steering Committee comprised of key power figures throughout the organization. In a nonunion setting, it should represent a diagonal slice of the organization's structure. In a unionized setting, it should include roughly an equal number of union and management leaders, but its overall size should be kept to twelve or fewer members if possible. This team must have the power and authority to allocate resources and make policy decisions when, and if, a change effort is launched. Members from management would vary, depending on the nature of the business, the number of functions and processes involved, the number of product or service lines, and the size of the organization. Membership on a Steering Committee might include:

- The highest ranking manager at the site (e.g., plant manager, president, or CEO)
- Someone from finance (e.g., CFO, manager of accounting)
- Someone from human resources
- Someone from engineering
- Someone representing middle management
- Someone representing first-line supervision

The union membership should include the president, chairperson of the Bargaining Committee, other committee members, and maybe some stewards. An hourly employee or two should be considered for committee membership, regardless of whether the company is unionized.

The Steering Committee should be responsible for all policy and strategic decisions regarding major organizational change efforts. These might include, but should not be limited to:

- Diagnosing the current health of the organization
- Establishing a vision of what the change should look like
- Setting objectives, policies, and local operating procedures
- Developing and/or approving plans, and subsequent adjustments, for the change effort
- Ensuring that resources, such as time, power, and money, in particular, are provided
- Modeling leadership conducive to the change effort

- Providing support through words and actions that will motivate and nurture the effort
- Monitoring and evaluating the impact of the change effort

The first task of the Steering Committee should be to conduct a diagnosis of the organization's overall health. This would include an environmental scan—gathering information regarding how customers, suppliers, the community, and other stakeholders external to the organization view it. Hard data regarding profitability, productivity, market share, quality, absenteeism, turnover, and grievance rates should also be examined. For example, is the organization achieving its objectives? What is the evidence for this? Surveys and interviews of a sample of employees representing a variety of organizational levels should also be conducted. What do employees think is working and not working? How satisfied are they with their jobs and their relationships with key players within the organization? Do they think there is a compelling need for change? What forces do they think are pushing for change? What forces do they think might hold back a change effort? All the hard data and the information from the environmental scan and the interviews should be summarized into four categories: (1) current strengths, (2) current weaknesses, (3) opportunities anticipated in the near future, and (4) anticipated threats to the organization's health.

The Steering Committee must make use of this data to determine if there is a need for change. If they think there is, then they must communicate this need to the rest of the organization. This is not necessarily an easy task. When top power players in an organization state that there is a need for change, certain reactions are likely to occur. Some will fear the message and assume that there is already a plan to eliminate jobs. Others will begin to look for scapegoats to ensure that they are not to blame for this need for change. Still others will attack the messengers, blaming them for the current state. Some will see this as an opportunity to win special favors for themselves. Many will ask, What's in this for me? Sending the message that there is a need for change legitimizes the venting of frustrations. Every past "sin" of management, and of the union, too, is likely to be revisited. At best, this venting will generate the energy to let go of the past and motivate efforts to do things differently in the future. Unfortunately, many change efforts never get past the venting stage. Once unleashed, employees may spend too much time justifying their anger over past mistakes. Once it becomes clear that 80 percent or so of the employees see a compelling need for change, the Steering Committee must move quickly to the second stage of organizational change: visioning.

Developing a Vision of What Could and Should Be

What kind of change would provide the strategy needed to address the problems of the current state of the organization and also the future threats and opportunities to it? At this point, it is important to know what options are available. Change can take many forms, such as reorganization, gainsharing plans, implementation of new technology, and teams. Since this book is about teams, we will only focus on the options utilizing teams. This may mean some form of team concept (e.g., the establishment of task forces, problem-solving teams, or self-directed work teams), but remember that many other popular organizational change efforts (e.g., total quality processes, gainsharing) also utilize teams as the basic unit of the new organization.

Who should identify these options and how are they to be discovered? The entire Steering Committee can attend a conference, read this book, or take some seminars together. An independent consultant can be hired to explain some options. Site visits of organizations that have successfully transformed themselves often prove to be energizing and enlightening. Sometimes the Steering Committee names a research team to identify and investigate the available options. The Research Team should include some members of the Steering Committee but could be utilized as another vehicle for getting people involved in the change process from the very beginning. Much of this depends on the size of the organization and the resources available. It is important to remember that at this stage, the focus is on finding the general thrust of what the change should look like. Detailed planning takes place after this initial investigation of options.

The Research Team/Steering Committee should consider no fewer than three options that might address the need for change determined in phase one. The pros and cons of these options must be researched. No option will be risk free, and none of the strategies will be perfect. If the team concept is one of the options to be considered, the committee should ensure that there are legitimate business reasons to consider the introduction of teams. Some of the reasons may be quite direct, for example, teams may be required to identify solutions to productivity problems due to the complex nature of the production process. Some of the reasons may be more indirect, for example, the diagnosis clearly indicates morale problems and this is costing the business through high absenteeism, grievance, or turnover rates. Whatever the reasons, teams should not be established simply for the sake of teams. Teams must be seen as a legitimate strategy to address the real problems currently facing the organization.

Ultimately, the Steering Committee must decide the direction the change effort is going to take. They must consider what will be different about the way things are done at the organization. They must paint a picture in words that addresses what the organization should and could be like. They must understand what milestones could be accomplished along the path of this change strategy. This vision is a broad-brush description of teams and how they can make a difference. When this vision is communicated with the rest of the organization, care should be exercised when making any promises. The vision should not be sold too strongly, at least not in any specific way. Promises and commitments must be followed through on or cynicism will erode any change effort. Expect What's in it for me? questions. Be prepared to turn that question back to employees and invite them to speculate on what could or should happen if the path is followed. The forums where the vision is announced might provide an opportunity to select members for the planning or Design Team who will do most of the work in the next phase of a successful organizational change.

If you thought that the announcement of the need for change would stir up problems and frustrations, wait until you announce the vision. Accusations that the organization failed to follow through on many other change efforts may surface. The words of the vision statement will be dissected, and implications never intended will be attributed to the effort. These reactions are not new. Machiavelli wrote in *The Prince* in 1513 that "it must be remembered that there is nothing more difficult to plan, more doubtful of success, nor more dangerous to manage than the creation of a new system. For the initiator has the enmity of all who would profit by the preservation of the old institution and merely the lukewarm defenders in those who would gain by the new ones." A well-written vision statement explains the basic notion of what kind of teams you want and why you want them. But this alone holds little significance. The vision statement will end up merely a slogan (and/or the butt of many jokes) unless a well-thought-out plan is also developed.

Drafting a Plan to Move Toward the Vision

A Design Team should be empowered by the Steering Committee to develop a detailed plan for how to make the vision of teams into a reality. The Design Team is often cochaired by two key players from the Steering Committee, but the remaining members must represent a vertical slice of the organization and the major functional areas as well. It is particularly important that people who are likely to be affected early on by a movement toward teams be represented on the Design Team. Some organizations hold elections for membership on the Design Team. More typically, members are appointed by top management and union leaders and approved by the entire Steering Committee on a consensus basis.

The Design Team has the very important and time-consuming task of coming up with a detailed plan on how to establish the team concept that the Steering Committee envisions. They must identify the steps to be taken, the rules for how teams are to be formed, the time frame to be followed, the necessary resources, the training to be offered, and all the remaining details. They are the "engineers" who provide the blueprint for the team concept. Their plan is subject to the approval of the Steering Committee. They need to address many questions that will contribute to this early preparation process. These questions should be addressed by any organization involved in this process and are included for your reference in exercise 1, "Preparing for Teams."

In addition to providing the details of this blueprint for teams, the Design Team is responsible for planning the events leading up to the launch of teams. What should be communicated to whom and by whom? When should this information be shared? What promises can be made? What "kickoff" events should be staged to let people know the change effort is a serious one? Will teams be established on a "wall-to-wall" basis or will pilot sites be attempted and then systematically spread through the facility?

The Steering Committee is the power umbrella to ensure that control and support exist, but the Design Team does much of the work. The Design Team will need some training and education to fulfill these tasks. It should be given the opportunity to visit other sites that have attempted a team concept. Generally speaking, Design Team members will need to attend seminars and workshops, and have access to a consultant. They should also be provided with team training themselves, and this may serve as a preview of the types of training opportunities that the work teams will ultimately be offered. Some design teams are expected to meet once or twice a week for two to four hours. That

EXERCISE 1

Preparing for Teams

Directions: The team responsible for providing a plan for the successful introduction of the team concept must first analyze the organization. Members should attempt to answer the following questions in order to identify strengths of the organization that will be capitalized on and problems that need to be resolved in order to make sure there is a realistic fit between the team concept and the organizational setting. Attempting to answer these questions will also generate a checklist of decisions to be made regarding how the team concept will be operationally defined at your location.

Developing a clear sense of direction

What will teams accomplish that is not currently being accomplished?

How will the teams be structured in order to ensure that each team is responsible for a whole, identifiable piece of work?

How will we know if a developed team is effective? What will each team be expected to accomplish? How will we measure team effectiveness? What measurable accomplishments will make up the scoreboard for each team to watch?

Having talented members

What knowledge/skills are needed to accomplish the goals expected of this team?

Does the right knowledge–skill mix to get the job done already exist on teams?

Who decides team membership? How will the membership of the teams reflect the Steering Committee's vision of a team (e.g., members of a single work unit, a whole operation, one shift, across shifts, problem-solving teams, or self-directed work teams)?

Who determines how to make use of the talent on the team?

How should a team acquire the needed knowledge or skills that are currently absent from the team?

Who is responsible for the skill development of team members?

What training should be offered to team members (e.g., training on job skills and on how to work together on teams)?

What training should be offered to managers, leaders, and resource people who will end up being key supporters of the team concept at this organization?

EXERCISE 1 continued

Establishing clear and enticing responsibilities

What responsibilities come with team membership (e.g., voluntary or mandatory attendance at team meetings, compliance with team decisions, and identification, resolution, and implementation of problems/solutions)?

Will each member be expected to fulfill more than one role on a team? Are team members expected to learn each other's jobs? Which responsibilities are to be shared? How?

Will the team have an assigned supervisor or area manager? What are the roles and responsibilities of this "leader"?

Will the team elect a group leader? What are the roles and responsibilities that this group leader is expected to fulfill?

Will the roles and responsibilities of the union steward who represents the members of the team change as a result of the development of the team?

Who is responsible for disciplinary action if the need arises?

Establishing reasonable and efficient procedures

How will jobs and tasks be assigned? Will members be expected to rotate among assignments?

How will shift and overtime preferences be handled?

What data will the team be expected to track? What data will the organization track for the team? What information will the team have access to? What reports or information is the team expected to provide to others in the organization?

Who is to convene team meetings? How often should a team meet? For how long? Should minutes be kept? Posted?

What problem-solving procedures should the team use (e.g., the 4-A method that will be explained in chapter 7)?

What decision-making procedures should a team use (e.g., consensus, majority rule)? Which decisions does the team have the authority to make? Which decisions require the team to provide recommendations to others who will make the final decisions?

What are the limits, financial and otherwise, that the team must keep in mind when problem solving/decision making?

What plans (e.g., schedules, work procedure changes) are teams expected or allowed to produce?

Are teams expected to gather data to monitor their own progress?

EXERCISE 1 continued

Developing constructive intepersonal relationships

What ground rules of personal behavior will be established to increase the likelihood that team members will show respect to each other? How will these ground rules be enforced?

Will time be set aside for team members to socialize or at least get to know each other better?

What help will teams receive to prepare them to handle conflict constructively? How should the team handle personality conflicts?

Will any symbols (e.g., banners, jackets, hats) be provided to emphasize team identity?

Ensuring reinforcement systems

Will a "pay-for-knowledge" agreement be used to reward members for learning each others' jobs?

Will any other team bonus system be established?

Will the supervisor's performance review reflect his or her ability to work with the team? Will any other formal performance reviews take place for anyone associated with developed teams?

Can ideas generated within developed teams be submitted to the proper channels in some kind of suggestions system?

How will recognition be provided to teams and their members?

Establishing constructive external relationships

Who is responsible to coordinate/facilitate team activities on a day-to-day basis? How?

What is the plan for gaining the support and commitment of middle-level managers and union leaders for the team development efforts?

Will team members directly interact with vendors, suppliers, and customers? How should this be handled?

Does any existing organizational system (e.g., promotion system, performance review system, purchasing, training) represent a threat or opportunity for teams as they begin to operate as a more developed unit? What should be done about this?

Will the establishment of teams create any possible violations of the union contract or accepted shop rules (e.g., seniority provisions, job classification schemes, rate classifications, overtime equalization provisions)? Will needed adjustments be negotiated at the local or national level? Will the provisions be attached as a Letter of Agreement? Will there be opportunities to try these provisions on a trial basis?

Will the physical facilities be modified to help the teams function more effectively?

means it may take several months to come up with the plan for teams at a particular location. Some companies put Design Team members on special assignment and allow them to spend most of their working hours developing the plan. Design Teams often form task forces made up of their own members so that several elements of the plan can be researched and developed simultaneously. All of this work is to prepare the organization for the advent of teams. The team members themselves also need to be prepared, which will be addressed in chapter 3.

Providing the Leadership and Support for the Changes

I must say that I have seen organizations go through the first three stages of this change model and still not succeed with the team concept. I have seen instances in which enough people saw the need for change, top leadership announced their vision for what the change process would be like, and a Design Team produced a step-by-step plan to move toward the vision, yet that plan only became part of a binder that sat on the shelves of managers or in someone's file drawers. Exciting off-site meetings were held and people were enticed to consider the need for teams. Some teams were declared, but then it was business as usual. Managers, and some union leaders, too, consciously or unconsciously, sabotaged the change effort by not adjusting their leadership style and by not sharing the decision-making power and responsibility needed for the teams to succeed. Chapter 6 will explore more thoroughly the changing roles of managers under a team concept. At this point, suffice it to say that unless the leaders of the organization support the plan approved by the Steering Committee, the likelihood of success is very low.

Champions of the team concept must take the initiatives/risks needed to activate the plan. Responsibilities must be shared without the usual efforts to find scapegoats if things should go wrong. A broader segment of the population must be given the opportunity to participate in the change process across time. This can upset vested interests and threaten the egos of leaders who have maintained their status through power and control rather than by encouraging commitment and ownership of the change process.

I will never forget one client, which had undergone a seemingly good experience with the first three stages of the change model. We were holding a meeting with all the organization's managers to gain their support and prepare them for the transitions ahead. Everyone seemed to be saying the right things: "People are our most important asset"; "We can trust our people to make the right decisions for the company"; "We all would be so much better off to have 350 people thinking instead of just having us thirty-five managers making the decisions." Everyone was saying these things except one individual who kept growling that this wouldn't work. He pointed to several previous failed change efforts and made sarcastic comments regarding the idealistic statements made by his fellow managers. During a break in the meeting, he pulled me aside and said, "Beware of the dudes!" I asked him what he meant. He said, "You know what a dude is, don't you?" I knew if I just hung in there a little longer he would explain it to me. He said, "A dude is someone who can dress up like a cowboy but doesn't know how to ride a horse." Now this was interesting to me. I figured out that he was warning me that his fellow managers could talk the right game about leading in a style conducive to teams, but that they didn't know how to ride that horse, so to speak. They could be friendly, but when it came to managing, they knew only one way to get things done—that is, give a directive and push people to get it done. They confused the participative style with just being friendly and idealistic. When routines were going smoothly, they appeared to be supportive of teams, but any other time, they expected to be in charge. They weren't ready to work with people. They were dudes rather than cowboys in riding the team approach to managing an organization.

To use this employee's analogy, if the ratio of dudes to cowboys is too high at your organization, you will also have a hard time taking teams seriously. The role of all managers will need to be clarified. Training will need to be offered to managers who lack the knowledge and skills needed to use a more participative style. Managers will ultimately have to join teams in which they can influence decisions at levels beyond their previous functional areas. The performance review and compensation systems must be applied consistently with the values underlying the change to a team concept. Still, some holdouts might refuse to change. How can this be dealt with? Will top-level management expect lower-level managers to act in a participative manner with teams of hourly employees but not involve their own direct reports in strategic planning teams and other top-level decision-making opportunities? Leadership and support for the change to a team concept must be provided symbolically through words and especially through actions. This typically takes time and always requires that a few brave souls demonstrate their true commitment to the process and the organization and ensure that such leaders are not only not punished but, rather, are positively recognized and rewarded.

The change to a team concept requires having a few friends in the right places. It requires leaders who have the knowledge, skills, and attitudes conducive to the change. It requires the opportunities to activate the plan, move toward the vision, and address the need for change.

Following Through on the Change Plan

People in most organizations today are likely to be cynical about an attempt to move toward a team concept. They may see the effort as the "personnel-program-of-the-month club entry." Many have attended off-site meetings and all-employee meetings before where management announced the latest and greatest fad effort that was supposed to turn everything around. Nearly all employees who have attended training sessions have reported that they were not encouraged or allowed to use what they had learned. Professionals today seem fine about putting on impressive events and exciting training programs, but the lack of follow-through appears to be an epidemic, wasting many opportunities, resources, and hope.

If the employees at your organization have witnessed a previous failed change effort or if enough employees admit to feeling a lack of trust in the organization and its management, action, not words, will be needed before any turnaround will occur. The key to building trust is consistency. It is crucial that actions back up the words people hear, that behaviors are consistent with espoused values, and that the steps of the change plan are operationalized. If input is sought, it must be utilized or explanations must be provided. Revisions to the plan will be required, but leadership must not flip-flop easily or frequently. At this point, top leadership must be adamant about its intentions to utilize teams as a main business strategy. The opportunity to turn back this process was during the development of the vision statement and in the design of the plans. It must be made clear that the winds are blowing in the direction of teams and that the only thing people can do now is learn how to adjust their sails to successfully guide the vehicle of teams toward the accomplishments expected of them. It is very important that the promises made during the launch of a team concept are delivered. It is important that Steering Committee members, the Design Team, trainers, and all leaders associated with the stages of the change effort make very small but clear promises and then make very visible efforts to fulfill those promises.

Summary

In order to prepare an organization for change, a clear need for change must first be established. Top leadership must draw a picture of what the organization should look like to address this need for change. Plans must be established to move the people and the systems associated with the organization toward the vision. Leaders must be willing to take the risks needed to activate the plan. Promises and commitments must be fulfilled. Actions must be consistent with the words and values of the change effort. Organizations taking teams seriously must set the stage appropriately. In the next chapter, we will turn our attention to the activities needed to help prepare the members of the teams themselves.

CHAPTER 3

Getting Team Members Ready for Change

The power and authority granted by the Steering Committee, the wisdom and insights of the Research Team, and the plans and time frame recommended by the Design Team all in place, it is time to establish effective and satisfying teams to produce the results needed to make the organization successful. Every team-building activity must be developed with two things in mind:

- There is a task to be accomplished by the team.
- The relationships between team members must be sufficiently respectful and satisfying.

Team-building activities must be task- and relationship-oriented. Assuming that the recommendations regarding the scope and structure of the teams has been approved by the Steering Committee, it is time to bring the members together and provide them with the tools needed to accomplish their mission.

Selecting Team Members

If the organization is brand new or if there is to be a total restructuring of the old organization, decisions must be made regarding who will be on which team. Members of new organizations are to be selected for their job skills, their technical potential, and their abilities to work as team players. Technical requirements should be identified by a thorough job analysis. Technical skills can be evaluated through performance tests. However, many companies believe that given a certain

level of physical dexterity and knowledge of the type of work to be performed, people can be trained to be technically proficient. Of greater
concern to many is whether the person will have the talent and attitudes needed to work together with others on a team. This primarily
involves interpersonal skills. Can the person share information in an
effective manner? Does the person have good listening skills? Can the
person provide constructive feedback? These and other behaviors are
probably best assessed through a combination of interviews and
small-group simulations.

Interview questions must not be leading or rhetorical. It is best to
begin with a very general question, for example, "What has been your
best experience with a team and how did you contribute to the team's
success?" Ask about hypothetical situations regarding what the person
would do if conflict arose in a group or if a team meeting was failing
to accomplish its purpose. See if the person is clear about what
strengths she or he could offer the team and what she or he will work
on improving over the next year. Allow the person to collect his or her
thoughts before answering your questions, otherwise, the interview
process may favor extraverts too much. Find out how well the person
practices systematic problem solving through small-group simulation
exercises. Try to notice whether the person defines the problem before
analyzing its causes. See if the person refrains from providing answers
before investigating causes. Observe whether the person abides by the
rules of brainstorming, especially in refraining from criticizing suggestions during the idea-generating period, and participates in coming
up with many solutions to the simulated problem. The most successful teams have a variety of personalities on them. Be careful that your
own biases toward outgoing, insightful individuals do not eliminate
the selection of more thoughtful, detailed-oriented team members.

If the selection is taking place in an already established firm, team
members (or at least a subset of them) are often involved in the selection process. In order to ensure that this works to your advantage,
make sure that these members are skilled at interviewing, understand
the basics of equal opportunity employment laws, are focused on the
knowledge and skills required of the members of the new team, and
are prepared to provide applicants with a realistic preview of what it
will be like to work on this team. Selection procedures must be reliable
and valid. It is important that members are not chosen simply because
they are likable. Information on job skills, work habits, interpersonal
skills, and team skills must be gathered as efficiently and consistently

as possible. The selection process should be documented and evaluated. Selectors should be reminded that the best predictor of future behavior is past behavior. So even though you are looking for potential, the ability of the applicant to describe the lessons she or he has learned from previous experiences should be given priority attention.

Assessing Teams for Development

Whether the teams are being launched in a new organization or relaunched in an existing one, a plan to develop the effectiveness of each team should be established. This means that two or three things must be accomplished:

- There should be a technical analysis of the jobs and tasks that the team is to accomplish.
- If it is an already existing team, an analysis of what the team does well and the things it collectively needs to do better or differently must be made.
- There should be a training needs assessment that determines the knowledge and skills of the individual team members.

Technical Analyses

In order to complete a job analysis, the organization—that is, top management in conjunction with the human resources, union leadership, and the engineering experts needed to conduct the analysis—must be clear about what part of the business each team is to accomplish. The production or service process would then be examined to identify the behaviors, technical knowledge, and skills needed for success. These job requirements are really needed to make valid selection decisions as well as to assess current employees for possible developmental opportunities. If you are just starting a new operation, the specific job requirements may not be known yet; you may need to bring together an assortment of experts to speculate on what these requirements might be and then adjust these based on the experience and input later gained by the team members once they are placed into these positions.

Time is a valuable resource. In order to make better use of the time dedicated to developmental opportunities offered to teams, a plan should be arranged that provides teams with meeting time to generate strategies for capitalizing on the strengths the team already has. Training and other developmental opportunities should be arranged to address the deficits the teams seem to have. This means that the teams must be assessed. This can be done through interviews, questionnaires, observation of team processes, and examination of team results. All of these methods can be used by a member or members of the team itself, depending on the trust levels that exist. Sometimes it is helpful to involve a professional who is outside of the team to gain some measure of confidentiality and objectivity. However, no matter how much expert help is provided, the members of the team itself must ultimately believe in the assessment data and make use of it.

Team Interviews

The purpose of team interviews is to see what, if any, assistance can be provided in order for the team to become a model of excellence. Such assistance needs to be tailor-made to fit the qualities of a team. Team members as well as key parties outside the team who are familiar with the accomplishments of the team and how it operates should be considered good sources of data. Interviews can be conducted on an individual, small subgroup, or total team basis. The main considerations are how much time is available to gather this assessment data and whether team members will be inhibited to open up and be honest in front of other team members. Regardless, while anything said by a given individual in these interviews should be utilized in the design of the developmental sessions, the source should remain confidential. The purpose is to look for the themes that emerge across interviews, not to communicate what was said by whom. A summary of the interview results should be written up and provided to all those who participated. Team members should be made aware of any plans to share this summary with anyone outside of the team. Sample questions for a team interview are provided in exercise 2, "Team Assessment Interview," for your reference.

Team Questionnaires

Confidential questionnaires completed by all the members of a team can also provide valuable data to be used to plan team development interventions. This can be used as a supplement to the interviews or by themselves as a quick and dirty assessment of existing teams. The questionnaire should cover the full range of components that constitute

EXERCISE 2

Team Assessment Interview

Directions: The following questions are to be asked of each team member (and some key players not on the team but knowledgeable of the team) by someone the team trusts. This person is to identify the themes that emerge from the answers provided and feed this information back to all participating interviewees. The source of the comments should be kept confidential. Instead of interviews, the team could meet and discuss each of these questions and develop their own assessment if a trusted interviewer is not available.

1. What do you think are the keys for great success in the use of a team approach to work and problem solving?

2. How effective and satisfying is this team? What are this team's greatest strengths?

3. What would you like to see this team do better or differently?

4. What would you like your teammates and/or the resource people serving your team to learn or relearn at development sessions?

5. What forces, obstacles, barriers, and sources of resistance will need to be overcome in order for your team to become great?

6. What forces exist that may push for greater success with your team?

7. What would you expect from me if I attempt to work with you and this organization to facilitate team excellence?

8. What should I be able to expect from you when working with your team?

9. What else should I know in order to be of help in the efforts to develop fully effective and satisfying teams?

what it takes to be an effective team. Beware of questionnaires that only ask about feelings and relationships while ignoring issues relevant to task procedures. Written questions can be of the fixed format or the open-ended variety. However, keep in mind that many people do not like to fill out detailed responses to open-ended questions, and these questions are probably best suited for the interview format. Several surveys are commercially available. If the survey has been pretested, has some reliability and validity evidence, and has some norms to help assess the results, it may be worth the expense.

My own "Team Diagnostic Questionnaire" is provided in exercise 3. It has been utilized with more than 100 teams and the scale scores all have respectable reliability and validity evidence. The norms for each of the questions are provided in table 3 on a form that you can use to provide feedback results to your team. You do not need to hire a professional to administer this questionnaire. However, you should make arrangements for all responses to be deposited with a trusted person who will compile the team averages for each item without revealing any individual's ratings.

Team Observation

Another way to assess the current effectiveness level of a team is to observe it in action. This offers the advantage of gathering data on how the team actually operates, not what team members report about themselves. This method can provide insights into how the team conducts meetings, keeps its members involved, systematically solves problems, goes about planning, and deals with conflict and other interpersonal issues. Thus, it provides data on team procedures and perhaps also interpersonal relations. The team observation method does have several disadvantages, however. When team members know they are being observed by an outsider, their behavior probably changes. They either act on their best behavior—especially the group leader—or they take the opportunity to complain to the observer or try to pull the observer into resolving a dispute or judging whether their approach to a situation is "right" or "wrong." If team members know that one of their own is attempting to observe the team to assess its level of development, their behaviors may again change. Even if they do not consciously make an effort to act differently, they may be observed on an unusual day. The group would need to be observed at least several times to obtain a good sample of their typical behavior. Observations can be useful, but interviews, questionnaires, and other data-gathering methods will be needed to supplement the observational data to address other issues such as goal and role clarity and team satisfaction.

It helps to have a checklist in front of you that addresses such issues when observing a group to ensure that the broad range of possible dynamics is attended to. It might also add some objectivity and eliminate the problem of merely seeing what one wants to see in the team.

EXERCISE 3

Team Diagnostic Questionnaire (Quick Scoring Form)

Directions: Each team member should complete this questionnaire. In order to help identify your team's strengths and weaknesses, honest and independent responses of every member of your team are needed. Each person's individual responses will be kept strictly confidential. Each individual will receive a copy of the team's average response to each question and how this team compares with a sample of other teams who have used this instrument.

Name of team: _____

For each of the following items, you will be asked, How true is the statement for your team now? For all items, circle the rating that is currently most accurate for the situation described regarding your team, with 0 = not at all, 1 = a little bit, 2 = somewhat, 3 = to a large extent, and 4 = very much.

1a. The goals of our team are appropriate and clearly stated.

    0   1   2   3   4

1b. The members of our team are committed to the accomplishment of our shared team goals.

    0   1   2   3   4

1c. Our team accomplishes its goals.

    0   1   2   3   4

2a. Our team collectively contains the full range of talents we need to be an effective unit.

    0   1   2   3   4

2b. The talents of the members of our team are fully utilized.

    0   1   2   3   4

3a. The role of leadership is competently fulfilled by one or more people on this team.

    0   1   2   3   4

3b. Each member of our team clearly understands the role he or she is to play for us to be an effective unit.

    0   1   2   3   4

EXERCISE 3 continued

3c. Each member of our team clearly fulfills the role he or she is expected to play.

    0   1   2   3   4

4a. Our team uses effective and efficient procedures to work together to complete our tasks.

    0   1   2   3   4

4b. Our team uses effective and efficient procedures to identify and resolve problems as they occur.

    0   1   2   3   4

4c. Our team holds effective and efficient meetings.

    0   1   2   3   4

4d. Our team uses effective and efficient procedures to ensure that information is shared and received.

    0   1   2   3   4

4e. Our team uses effective and efficient planning procedures.

    0   1   2   3   4

4f. Our team effectively monitors its progress.

    0   1   2   3   4

5a. Our team members deal with conflict in a constructive manner.

    0   1   2   3   4

5b. Our team members provide enough support to each other to encourage a sense of belonging to the team.

    0   1   2   3   4

5c. Team members provide enough positive challenge to each other to encourage high levels of performance.

    0   1   2   3   4

5d. Team members get along with each other quite well.

    0   1   2   3   4

6a. Team members provide each other with enough recognition for our working together as a team.

    0   1   2   3   4

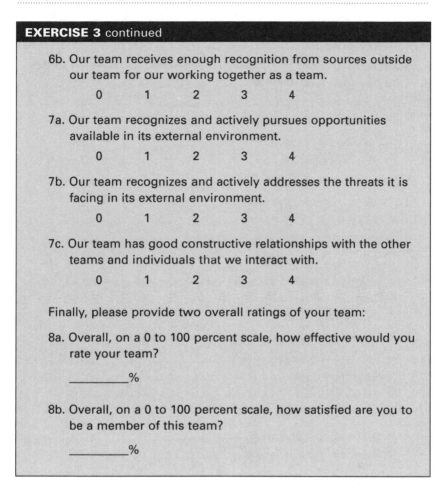

EXERCISE 3 continued

6b. Our team receives enough recognition from sources outside our team for our working together as a team.

0   1   2   3   4

7a. Our team recognizes and actively pursues opportunities available in its external environment.

0   1   2   3   4

7b. Our team recognizes and actively addresses the threats it is facing in its external environment.

0   1   2   3   4

7c. Our team has good constructive relationships with the other teams and individuals that we interact with.

0   1   2   3   4

Finally, please provide two overall ratings of your team:

8a. Overall, on a 0 to 100 percent scale, how effective would you rate your team?

_____%

8b. Overall, on a 0 to 100 percent scale, how satisfied are you to be a member of this team?

_____%

When I have been asked to observe a team "because they are having a lot of conflict," it is hard not to interpret all actions as signs of conflict. Exercise 4, "Analyzing Group Processes," provides a checklist of key things for you to look for in a group setting.

Observation helps us to see what a team is doing, but it does not verify why it is doing it in a particular manner. That is why the feedback of team observation data is so important. Here, perhaps more than any other method, one must remember that assessment is actually an intervention itself. Care must be exercised not to stir up desire for change that is more extensive than will be permitted by the Steering Committee. While you want to verify that the group feels that

Table 3 *Team Diagnostic Questionnaire* Results

Questionnaire Items	Your Group	Comparison Groups
1a. Clear and appropriate goals	_____	2.26
1b. Commitment to goals	_____	2.44
1c. Accomplishes goals	_____	2.26
2a. Full range of talents	_____	2.81
2b. Full use of talents	_____	1.99
3a. Leadership role fulfilled	_____	2.60
3b. Clear understanding of roles	_____	1.95
3c. Each role fulfilled	_____	1.99
4a. Work procedures	_____	1.97
4b. Problem-solving procedures	_____	1.98
4c. Meeting procedures	_____	1.97
4d. Communication procedures	_____	2.03
4e. Planning procedures	_____	1.92
4f. Progress monitoring procedures	_____	1.82
5a. Conflict handled constructively	_____	1.92
5b. Support provided to each other	_____	2.06
5c. Challenge provided to each other	_____	1.90
5d. Get along well	_____	2.57
6a. Peer recognition provided for team	_____	2.08
6b. External recognition for team	_____	1.46
7a. External opportunities pursued	_____	1.83
7b. External threats addressed	_____	1.97
7c. Constructive external relations	_____	2.02
8a. Overall effectiveness rating	_____	65%
8b. Overall satisfaction rating	_____	75%

there is a need for change, you do not want to make promises—inferred or explicit—that will not be met. Table 4 provides a step-by-step approach for how to report back a group observation to a team. Notice that this method combines assessment with an opportunity for the team to develop changes in its approach to working together. It is an approach that can be used by external as well as internal observers.

EXERCISE 4

Analyzing Group Processes

Directions: Use the questions provided in the checklist below to insure that the broad range of possible dynamics are looked for during your observation of a team. Familiarize yourself with this checklist in advance so that you do not miss noticing these things if they arise. Table 4 will provide you with specific step-by-step instructions on how to feed back your observations to the team in a manner that promotes constructive change.

1. Participation levels

Who participated the most? The least? How were the silent members treated? Were there any shifts in participation levels? Who talked to whom?

2. Leadership

Who had the most influence? Over which issues?

How did various members gain influence?

Who would you say was the *task* leader?

Who would you say was the *social* (relationship oriented) leader?

3. Group roles

Who would you say played which of the following task-oriented roles: Idea initiator? Information/opinion giver? Coordinator? Topic gatekeeper? Consensus tester? Clarifier/summarizer? Task accomplishment evaluator?

Who would you say played which of the following social (relationship oriented) roles: Harmonizer? Person gatekeeper? Encourager/support giver? Team spirit captain? Team member relations evaluator?

Who would you say played which of the following dysfunctional roles: Avoider? Dominator? Attention seeker? Dependent member? Blocker? Attacker? Clown? Standards reducer? Topic jumper? One upper?

4. Decision-making procedures

What styles of group decision making were used: Self-authorized? Handclasp? Majority rule? Compromise? Consensus?

Did the group openly decide how it would make its decisions?

EXERCISE 4 continued

5. Group norms and sanctions

Were ground rules stated? What "rules" (spoken and unspoken) influenced how the group actually worked? What norms were established regarding standards of performance? Group cohesion? Risk taking? What rewards and punishments were used to maintain the group's norms? (Hint: Look for subtle clues, including uses of humor.) What rewards and punishments were used to reinforce changes in the behavior of group members?

6. Group heterogeneity

How did the group celebrate/capitalize on the differences that existed between its members? To what extent did this group make full use of its human resources?

7. Group procedures

Did the group clarify the purpose and agenda for the meeting? Did it follow the agenda? Did the group follow a systematic approach to problem solving? Did the group assign responsibilities to particular individuals to ensure that actions would be taken on decisions made by the group? How was this handled? Did the group manage its time well?

8. Group effectiveness

How well did this group do on its task? Overall, what are the strengths and weaknesses of this group?

Providing Training

Practitioners believe that training is the key resource that must be provided to succeed with the team concept (Wellins et al., 1991). The training may include sessions on the technical knowledge and skills needed to succeed on the job. Sessions on how to operate the equipment, troubleshoot, read key charts and reports, perform the jobs originally performed by other team members, and understand the business' budgeting, scheduling, and purchasing processes should be provided early in the launch process but only when the team members can practice what they are learning on the job.

Training sessions on interpersonal and team skills can be provided in many formats. Chapters 4 through 10 provide many examples of

Table 4 Providing Group Process Feedback

Initiate in a manner that isn't disruptive and is desired.

Seek permission to provide feedback, for example, "Would you be interested in hearing what I see going on in the group?"

Solicit the group's perceptions first.

Let the group own up to its own behaviors, for example, "What do you notice about what is going on with the group now?"

Describe what you saw going on in nonevaluative terms.

Focus the group's attention on a specific example or pattern that you feel is going on in the group. Don't overload the group and don't become its judge or evaluator. For example, you might say, "What I saw happening was...." or "What I heard X say was...."

Seek verification of your perception.

Find out if the group now agrees with what you said was going on, for example, "Did anyone else see or hear that?"

Clarify implications of the dynamic that is identified or verified.

Ask the group to figure out the impact of the behavior or pattern now that the group has verified that it did occur. What effect has the dynamic caused? For example, you might say, "Now that we agree that this pattern exists, what impact does it have on the group's ability to perform?"

Build a commitment to change.

Bring the discussion to a conclusion by getting the group to figure out how it is going to capitalize on the dynamic or how it is going to operate to avoid repeating the pattern or behavior. For example, "What should we do if this occurs again? What are the alternative ways of dealing with this dynamic and who will take responsibility for initiating the alternative approach?"

Reinforce the effort to change and any positive results that will arise from it.

Thank the group for taking the time to look at itself. Encourage the group to continue its efforts to become more effective. Provide recognition, either privately or publicly, when group members follow through on their commitments to attempt to deal with the dynamic more effectively.

---

exercises and team sessions in which members can attain the clarity needed to work together on the team and the skills required. Typical topics in these team skills sessions include communication, conflict resolution, planning, decision making, conducting meetings, making presentations, sharing leadership, and problem solving. Sessions might also emphasize understanding one's own and one's teammate's personalities, the hidden talents of teammates, and perceptions of key managers and of systems that could support efforts to make the team successful.

Common Mistakes Made in Providing Team Training

While training is indeed important, many training dollars and opportunities are also often wasted in this area. In their eagerness to show support for the team concept, managers and union leaders often agree to spend money and find the time for team members to attend training sessions. However, the following section outlines the mistakes often made in offering training for team development (Huszczo, 1990).

Starting Team Training Without First Assessing Team Needs

Why make people learn skills that they already have? Why not honor and respect the knowledge and skills that already exist on the team and the fact that team member time is valuable? You won't know what the training should focus on unless you conduct a training needs assessment (TNA) beforehand. Without a prior assessment, trainers are likely to use a shotgun and/or canned approach to team training. Many managers might think, Well, it won't hurt any of them to go through the whole thing. However, one size does not fit all. It may be comforting to the trainer and convenient for the organization to provide the exact same program to every team, but this will not provide the opportunity to maximize the impact of the training on the team's performance. Remember, the purpose of the training should not merely be to take credit for providing training. To develop and grow effective teams, you need to ensure that the training fits the developmental needs of the team.

Despite the logic of utilizing a TNA, there are various forces within most organizations that could easily inhibit trainers from insisting on doing a TNA. Some may fear that the very act of asking team members how well their team is doing may stir up conflict. In addition, many trainers have much better presentation and facilitation skills than they do the data gathering and analysis skills needed to conduct a TNA. For that matter, no one can perfectly measure team satisfaction and effectiveness or precisely determine how well each member can utilize team skills. Companies may hesitate when considering the additional cost of doing a TNA, and an external trainer who insists on it may lose his or her bid for the work.

Nevertheless, without the benefit of any preexisting data, it will be difficult to determine whether team effectiveness actually did improve after training. Not looking into the team knowledge and skills before a program begins is like pretending that team members don't know anything about teams before they begin the training. It's as if we send people to these magic sessions and some person external to the team, a trainer, fixes the team. Experience is a wonderful teacher, and we don't need training sessions if experience has already taught us the lessons we need to know. Identifying what team members have already learned and then designing a session to determine how to make use of what experience has taught them can be very valuable and empowering. The TNA interviews can also help reduce fears about the upcoming team concept intervention, share information about the plans for teams, hype the team-building sessions, and allow a facilitator to get acquainted with team members and establish expectations. TNAs are very likely to be worth the expense if one is dealing with existing teams.

Confusing Team Building With Teamwork

While a main purpose of team training is to help people learn how to work together, team building is more than teamwork. Too often, sessions overemphasize getting people to be happy and able to get along with others. Of course, it is more desirable to be on a team in which members get along, but you could be left with a team that produces mediocre work and uses mediocre group processes. All team efforts must be task *and* relationship oriented. When team training sessions overemphasize relationship building, many members will not take teams seriously. They will see the whole team concept as "soft" and not bottom-line oriented. Overemphasis on happiness and getting along with others will appear to some as brainwashing sessions aimed at eliminating complaining. Granted, it is wearing to have a whole team full of people who complain too much, but this conflict at least shows that people care enough to speak their minds. The opposite of conflict is apathy, not peace and harmony. Learning how to deal with conflict constructively is an important goal of some team training efforts; chapter 8 will address this issue more thoroughly. The point is that the best approach to developing teams must include a balance of task- and relationship-oriented activities.

Failing to Use a Systematic Model
to Plan Team Development Activities

An overemphasis on task rather than relationship building is also a mistake. Teams may need technical training (e.g., job skills, system knowledge), process skills (e.g., how to hold effective meetings, solve problems, reach consensus decisions), and/or relationship-building skills. The data gathered during the TNA must cover the full range of components needed to have an effective team. Trainers can best serve teams by using a systematic model of team effectiveness like the one described in chapter 1. The model serves as a basis for the TNA, for the design of the sessions, and for subsequent evaluation. A model provides for a disciplined approach to team development. It helps avoid some of the problems already described and the problem many trainers have of overusing their favorite team development technique. There is an old Chinese proverb that roughly translates to mean, "If your only tool is a hammer, all your problems will begin to look like nails." Using a model of team effectiveness increases the chances that you will be thorough and systematic in your approach to developing teams.

Assuming Teams Are Basically All Alike

You certainly wouldn't provide the same training regimen to a baseball team as you would a basketball team. Our approach to team concepts for work teams should be as diverse as would be used in different sports. In his book, *Game Plans*, Robert Keidel (1985) points out that different sports strategies fit certain organizations better than others. His ideas could be extended to work teams as well.

For example, according to Keidel, some work units are like baseball teams, where each member is allowed to act fairly independently of the others. The first baseman rarely knows exactly what the left fielder is doing, unless there is a play from left field to first base, in which case they work very closely together. Certain key figures need to be in constant communication, for example, the pitcher and the catcher, while many other players communicate infrequently. Team members come to bat one at a time in baseball, not unlike salespeople who are part of a team but make calls and close sales by themselves. Occasionally, they need to understand (or at least could benefit from understanding) what other members of the sales force are doing in order to develop a more effective team effort.

Some teams in organizations are more like football teams, according to Keidel. A football team must move incrementally forward. Success for a football team demands coordination across many different parts of the team. Some work teams, like those in mass-production situations, must have a lot of coordination across different units. Each member must move in a synchronized pattern, directed by a "coach" or "quarterback," who may seek input in the huddle but calls the final shots to help the team move forward effectively.

Still other work teams, says Keidel, model the strategies of basketball teams. A basketball team has players in constant interaction with each other. Certain team members are counted on to deliver certain skills (e.g., rebounding, passing, shooting) more than others, but all members must know all of the necessary tasks because change is rapid. A basketball team must be able to instantly switch from offense to defense without going into the dugout or a huddle. Many self-directed work teams must operate in a similar manner. The training implications for basketball teams are quite different than they are for football or baseball teams.

Even teams that are playing the same "sport" should not necessarily be coached and developed in the same manner. If a team has more new members than veterans, training may need to focus on the skills needed to improve quality rather than efficiency. If a key team member has a strong need for power and competition, the coach may need to develop opportunities for that player to channel his or her competitiveness externally (e.g., in negotiating with suppliers) rather than with teammates. Teams need training and strategies to capitalize on the unique talents, personalities, organizational situations, and task assignments they are expected to face. Trainers must work with the Steering Committee to know what those expectations are before designing developmental sessions in order to ensure that the training will be useful.

Sending Team Members to Team Training Individually Rather Than Collectively

It is very difficult to schedule training sessions for busy team members. Some organizations decide to send members separately to training sessions and ask the other members to manage the workload while they are away. There is an equality of sacrifice involved here. However, it assumes that people only need the knowledge of team dynamics and the skills to utilize their knowledge and observations. That approach works occasionally, but much of the activity involved in team development is the interplay of working through concepts together. The whole is greater than the sum of the parts, and time is needed to examine and determine how the parts fit together.

It is far better to have team members all attend the core training sessions together. This way, they all have the same information and, assuming the sessions are interactive, they can be asked to decide as a group how they are going to apply what they are learning back on the job. If business schedules make this impossible and members must attend sessions separately, meetings should be held to keep the message and team cohesive. Such meetings should (1) confirm what common knowledge was gained at the training sessions, (2) identify the implications of that knowledge for improving the effectiveness of the team, and (3) ask each member to make clear statements about their commitment to action that will apply the knowledge they've learned in the team training. Thus, the real team development occurs at the meeting and, subsequently, on the job. The team training is preparation for team development.

Failing to Hold Teams Accountable for Following Through and Using Their Training

Many managers and union leaders, that is, Steering Committees, appear to be unaware of what will actually occur during the training sessions. They seem to want to fulfill their pledge to provide training, receive positive feedback that people like the training sessions, and rest assured that it is not costing too much. They often make no clear arrangements regarding who will be responsible for ensuring follow-through on the points covered in the training. Trainers may need to take on this responsibility to ensure that the teams and the organization are prepared to follow through on what is learned and agreed to.

Who will have the responsibility to monitor implementation of team development plans and decisions? How will the team reward compliance or punish ignorance of its plans and efforts to put the training to use? Trainers need to build alliances within the organization to ensure that training is not a one-shot phenomenon. It needs to be made clear to team members that there needs to be a return on the investment of training dollars. Team members need to realize that they are responsible not only to show up at the sessions but also to attempt to apply what they learn.

Once team members establish a plan of action to use the procedures they heard or experienced during the training sessions, they need to consciously adopt a disciplined approach to applying their learning back on the job. Line managers need to help remove obstacles to these application attempts. Managers and union leaders need to "catch people doing things right." They need to keep a nurturing eye on the team and reinforce efforts by members to attempt the changes designed to make things better. Effort as well as results need to be rewarded if the team is to be effective. Thus, key leaders must get more involved with understanding and approving the materials and techniques to be covered in the team training sessions. If they don't understand it themselves, it will be difficult for them to be aware of and reward the application of it. Training must provide tools to team members. When an organization purchases tools, it should be prepared to ensure that those tools are put to use.

Too often, we have let teams off the hook too easily. When team members are asked what they gained from training, common responses include: "We got to know each other better," "We learned that we need to communicate more with each other," and "We learned that no one is perfect and we just need to accept each other." Such safe (i.e., socially desirable), broad statements are difficult to follow up on. We need dedicate time to helping teams draw up concrete statements of expectation before they leave their training sessions. We need to help teams identify who will do what with whom and by when in order to "communicate more with each other," or whatever general outcome is sought. Trainers will need to manage training time well enough so that teams do not have to rush through the opportunity to negotiate commitments. The team may even need to establish their own "enforcer" or enforcing mechanism so that people are reminded of their commitments to change. For a team to grow and develop, behaviors must change, and change is always a risk. The temptation will exist to let things slide and try to just hang on to some good feelings. If we are going to build effective teams, we need good feelings, behavioral changes, and recognition for follow-through.

Treating Team Building as a Program Rather Than a Process

Teams are sometimes sent to a two-, three-, or even five-day training program and the organization expects that years of habits will be changed for years to come. This again is an example of expecting training to create magic. Research clearly indicates that distributed practice, that is, shorter sessions spread across time, results in more of a long-term retention of learning than does massed practice, that is, one long cram session. A professional sports team would not hold all of its practices before the start of a season and then assume that it could operate effectively through all its games that season without having another practice. Some recreation league teams might try that because they don't consider the work they are doing as a team as important as their regular jobs. But are you going to treat your work teams as professional sports teams or as recreation league teams?

For that matter, I'm not even sure that team development actually occurs during team training sessions. Perhaps it really occurs back on the job as the members attempt to interact more effectively with each other and apply what they learned. Team training is bought and treated as programs. As a result, people see a beginning and an end to the team development activity. When the training ends, so does development, and then it is back to business as usual. Maybe things get extended somewhat. If an action plan is developed at the end of the team training program, development might end whenever the action plan can be either ignored or fulfilled. Training and action plans are often treated as activities to be checked off a list. Real development occurs across time and must be nurtured. It actually is never completed. It is a continuous improvement process, not unlike the tending of a garden.

Another sign that training is being treated as a program rather than as a process is when trainees can remember the jokes the trainer told or the artificial exercises that were completed or the wall they had to climb, but fail to remember the point of the stories or activities. The games and exercises are valuable in that they gain people's attention. Attention is a prerequisite to learning. It is necessary but not sufficient. The event must be synthesized into insights that must be translated into actions, and then the actions must be reinforced. When this process takes place, team training results in more effective teams.

Relying on Training Alone to Develop Effective Teams

Teams do not operate in a vacuum. Teams are part of a system and the parts of any system interact with each other and with their environment. What goes on in training should influence performance appraisal systems and vice versa. It should affect reward, information, and selection systems. Human resource professionals, or any change agents, need to utilize training as a springboard for many other interventions that prepare organizations for enhanced use of improved teams. Areas that should be explored include organization development (OD) techniques such as gainsharing plans, sociotechnical systems applications, survey-feedback interventions, total quality processes, and organizational restructuring. The Steering Committee needs to be educated on these options and decide if these OD techniques could be useful allies in efforts to enhance organizational effectiveness through team development.

Not Getting the Ground Rules Straight at the Beginning

It is unfair to get team members to share ideas and perceptions and then later punish them for opening up. If you are attempting to use teams to eliminate jobs, the people being asked to participate in this endeavor should know what they are involved in. If people are expected to use what they are learning in training, this should be made clear at the outset. Motivation is, in part, a function of expectations. Ground rules help people understand how they are expected to behave and provide for a more disciplined approach to team development sessions. Some ground rules that have been found to help people take team training sessions more seriously include having:

- Each member attend all sessions unless excused by all other members and then having him or her abide by any decisions agreed to by the group
- All team decisions be made by consensus rule
- A rule that no member is to criticize another member as a person; criticisms are to be directed at ideas, not people
- No side conversations; only one person can speak at a time during these sessions, except during exercises that use subgroups
- Each member attempt to apply what she or he is learning
- Any discussions during team-building sessions kept confidential; only consensus decisions are to be shared with anyone outside the team
- No one share the team diagnostic data results without permission of the whole team
- Each member attempt to share information, concerns, opinions, and questions in a manner that demonstrates respect for the team and its efforts to become a model team
- Each member listen to all comments made during the team-building sessions
- Team members provide the facilitator and their peers with feedback in a constructive manner, including making a genuine effort

to describe what one is responding to before offering any judgment of ideas

■ No retribution for statements made during team-building sessions
■ Sessions begin and end on time

Ground rules should be discussed at the very beginning of the team development sessions. Rules need to be agreed on or imposed. Whatever is decided must be made clear and followed. It is important to reinforce positive efforts to comply as well as "punish" behaviors that violate the rules. Punishment is typically limited to verbal reminders and a request to either comply with or decide to change the rule.

Having the Outside Facilitator/Consultant Lead the Team During the Training Sessions Instead of the Group

While it is common for a trainer to be at the front of the training room, it should also be made clear that the trainer is not the leader of the group. Trainers need to build alliances with team leaders if they exist. The trainer can provide information, state instructions for group exercises, facilitate discussions, and provide process observations. However, they need to help the leader enhance his or her abilities to fulfill the leadership role within the team. There are several things that the group leader can do that will help the team training be more effective. Table 5 summarizes what leaders can do to help in this process at various points in a training session.

Designing Effective Team Training Sessions

As was detailed in the previous section, there are many pitfalls to avoid in designing team training sessions. Each effort should be tailored to the target team. However, certain principles are likely to help in the design of training sessions to make a difference. Those principles include:

■ Conducting a systematic assessment of the team using the Seven Key Components of Effective Teams prior to the training sessions
■ Creating a disciplined design for each session that includes diagnosis, discussion, planning, experimentation, and reinforcement
■ Placing an emphasis on experience as the "real teacher" of adults and thus providing the team with the time to talk through issues

Table 5 How Leaders Can Help Make Training Sessions More Effective

Before the sessions

Encourage your group to have high expectations about this opportunity to bring up and discuss issues relevant to your team's effectiveness.

Clarify the expectations that all members are to attend and actively participate in the sessions.

Clarify any dress code expectations.

During the sessions

Practice your leadership skills by facilitating team discussions and exercises.

Attempt to motivate your team to get the most out of every opportunity the sessions provide.

Ask for feedback about your leadership style.

Provide positive reinforcement to members who constructively take the necessary risks that may propel your team to greater effectiveness.

Model the types of behaviors you would like to see your team's members demonstrate (e.g., sharing, listening, punctuality, taking on assignments, providing feedback).

Between the sessions

Remind team members about the behavioral "experiments" agreed to during the sessions. Ask if you can help them in their efforts to fulfill their commitments.

Fulfill the commitments you agreed to in the sessions.

Attempt to motivate team members to look forward to the next session.

After the sessions

Take any opportunity to remind your team that team development is an ongoing process and the responsibility of everyone involved.

Review your team's plan for excellence with your supervisor.

Reinforce group or individual efforts to act in a more team-oriented manner.

Ensure that the team takes the time to periodically monitor its progress.

---

and decide what to do rather than listen to lectures delivered by the trainer

- Continually using the key relationship-building skills of sharing, listening, and providing feedback
- Holding sessions off-site, away from the distractions of the job and scheduling enough time in between to allow experiments to be attempted and reinforced
- Allowing ample opportunities for leaders within teams to practice their skills by facilitating the discussions, rather than being led by an external instructor

- Allowing ample opportunities to receive feedback regarding the team's dynamics as observed by the trainer
- Using a measurement instrument to assist the team in monitoring its own progress in the months ahead
- Making clear statements about the objectives and ground rules that will focus the team training sessions

The objectives of such sessions should be stated in advance and are subject to negotiation. Proposed objectives for team building sessions might include some or all of the following:

- Develop this team into a model of how the best teams should function like in this organization.
- Identify and build commitment toward the shared goals that this team is to strive to achieve.
- Identify how individual goals of team members will contribute toward the enhancement of the overall team.
- Inventory the talent of the team and develop a plan to put the talent to use.
- Clarify the roles and responsibilities of each team member and clarify the willingness of each team member to fulfill these roles and responsibilities.
- Use a systematic problem-solving approach to enhance the effectiveness and efficiency of the procedures this team will use to operate together.
- Develop an understanding and appreciation of the personalities of team members and how to benefit from the diversity of styles that exist on this team.
- Enhance the ability of team members to deal constructively with conflict.
- Establish a commitment in each team member to reinforce team-oriented behaviors in other team members.
- Develop a plan to enhance the relationship between this team and key players and teams external to it.
- Establish an action plan to operationalize and sustain any and all progress gained through these team-building sessions.

State and negotiate the objectives of the training sessions first and then provide an outline of the agenda. Remember, the purpose of training is to enhance knowledge and skills, not to provide a set number of hours of training. The agenda would obviously vary, depending

Table 6 Sample Team-Building Session Agendas

Session # 1

Establish expectations

Feed back the diagnosis of the current state of the team through interviews and TDQ results

Identify the shared goals of this team

Establish a clear sense of direction

Celebrate the personalities of this team using information gained from the MBTI inventory

Inventory the talent of this team and plan its use

Develop a plan to personally help this team become more effective and/or more satisfying

Session # 2

Review efforts to fulfill the team's action plans

Examine the fulfillment of the leadership function on this team

Clarify the roles and responsibilities of each member of this team

Enhance the conflict resolution skills of this team

Session # 3

Improve the team's procedures to solve problems, make decisions, hold meetings, manage time, share and receive information, and develop work procedures

Establish a reinforcement system for team-oriented behaviors

Session # 4

Develop a plan to improve this team's external relations

Establish a strategic plan for team excellence

Follow-up session

Verify follow-through on plans and commitments

Celebrate progress

Adjust the plans where necessary

---

on which objectives are to be accomplished. Table 6 provides a sample agenda that has been used for a team that needed to address virtually all of the objectives listed in the previous discussion. This involved four one-day sessions spread across a six-week period and a one-day follow-up session three months later. The exercises and activities associated with the agenda items listed in table 6 appear throughout the next seven chapters of this book.

Summary

If you are going to build effective teams, you cannot simply declare them to be teams without providing the time and resources needed to nurture and develop their effectiveness. For new teams, this begins with a careful system for selecting team members. For existing teams, this calls for doing a systematic needs assessment before designing the team training sessions. This chapter described the methods for conducting such an analysis as well as sample interview, survey, and observation questions. Ten common pitfalls of team training sessions were described and sample objectives, agenda items, ground rules, and design principles were also provided. Team success is essentially a function of abilities, motivation, and opportunities. Team training sessions are opportunities to develop abilities, that is, knowledge and skills. We should not count on team training alone to enhance team effectiveness. Team members must be motivated to apply what they learn and decide on during the team training sessions. Developing effective and satisfying teams is a process, not a program. A commitment to monitor and enhance the Seven Key Components of Effective Teams must be provided and fulfilled. The next seven chapters will look at each of these components in detail and provide suggestions that will enable teams to do just that.

PART TWO

The Seven Key Components of Effective Teams

The next seven chapters provide the main course for this book. Each of the seven components for effective teams introduced in chapter 1—clear direction, talented members, clear and enticing responsibilities, reasonable and efficient operating procedures, constructive interpersonal relationships, active reinforcement systems, and constructive external relationships—will be examined in depth. Together they provide a systematic path to team excellence. If you are using this book to help a particular team, the assessment of the team will tell you which of these chapters deserve more of your attention. In addition to explanations of each component, exercises will be provided to help you help the team be effective. If you are a human resources professional, a trainer, or an organizational development consultant, you are probably well aware of how to modify and use these exercises. If you do not have such a background, the following suggestions will help you use this section of the book more effectively:

- *Explain why you believe the activity could be useful for the team.* State the purpose and how that purpose is relevant to the assessment conducted prior to the team-building sessions. Ask whether the team members are committed to trying the activity. Without at least this level of commitment, the likelihood of improvement is low.

- *Arrange the seating to minimize any status differences.* Thus, placing chairs or desks in a circle would probably be better than having people sit classroom style with one person at the front of the room.

- *Encourage people to be honest and everyone to participate.* Most of the exercises are designed to help members take a systematic look at what is going on. It is unreasonable to assume that everyone will participate at exactly the same level. However, if you open the session up for anyone to speak, expect certain team members to dominate the session. While you do not want to halt all such urges to speak out, you can equalize the playing field by suggesting a process in which you go around the group and allow each person to contribute their perspective on key questions. If a given individual wants to pass when it is his or her turn, let them do so unless you find that the person passes every time she or he has an opportunity to speak. In such cases, the individual may need to be encouraged or confronted in private to determine if she or he is failing to follow through on the commitment to try.

- *Ask someone to record key insights identified by the team.* It is best to record these insights on a surface that everyone can read at the same time (e.g., a flip chart, a blackboard, an overhead). This will help ensure that everyone is focusing on the same things and will probably help reduce the number of redundant comments. This may also focus the group on what the issues are rather than who is to blame for them.

- *Ensure that enough time is reserved to examine what was learned through the activity.* Remember, the purpose is not to go through the activity; it is to identify what the group needs to do to become a more effective and satisfying team. Thus, it is usually not enough to make general statements about what is to be learned such as "We need to communicate better." Learning needs to be translated into actions, for example, "Who is going to do what with whom in order for us to get better on this dimension of teams?" Encourage team members to be specific and to only make promises that they are going to be able to fulfill.

- *Plan for the end of each session to be the beginning of efforts to transfer the learning.* Close team-building sessions with a decision regarding when the team will meet again to assess whether the commitments have been fulfilled and whether the team improved as a result.

There are many, many ways to peel an orange (I promised a team at a Humane Society Chapter that I would no longer say, "There is more than one way to skin a cat."), and likewise, there are a multitude of ways to build effective teams. The exercises and activities provided in chapters 4 through 10 are testimony to this and have all been successfully used by teams in work organizations. However, the list of references at the back of this book will provide you with additional sources to consider. Before we begin our look at each component, let's take a look at an example of a facility that made a serious effort to establish effective self-directed work teams.

Case Study

Launching Self-Directed Work Teams in a Manufacturing Facility

A decision was made to establish self-directed work teams (SDWTs) at a Big Three auto plant that made car components. The company had had some success with employee involvement in problem-solving teams over the last ten years and believed that the many years of experience of its hourly workforce should be viewed as an asset, not a liability. The new plant manager sat down with the manufacturing manager who was responsible for approximately one-half of the production generated at this plant of 450 people. Together with the union bargaining chairperson, they envisioned a grand experiment that would allow employees to choose their own teams, adjust the rules as they saw fit, and revolutionize the production process. As you may know, job security is always a concern in plants that produce component parts, even when that plant is a wholly owned facility. The managers knew that if this effort failed, their careers could be finished. The union leader knew that if this failed, the plant could be shut down. But they had a deep faith in the plant's employees and decided to give it a try.

They convinced the corporation that this "team thing" would position the plant to produce the next generation of products. They convinced the administrators of the corporate-level Joint Training Fund to provide the necessary money to prepare the plant for the advent of teams. They went about the preparation in a first-class and dramatic fashion. They brought approximately 250 hourly and salaried employees off site several times and shared confidential information regarding the potential of the next generation product.

The union and management leadership described their vision of self-directed work teams. They publicly committed their support for this team concept. They set up a structure that included a Steering Committee that was empowered to make policy decisions. They negotiated the necessary Letters of Agreement to contractually allow for the existence of teams. They had the departments elect representatives to a Research Team that visited three facilities known to have succeeded with SDWTs. They asked the employees themselves to decide where the lines of demarcation should be to establish the departmental teams. Each departmental team elected a representative who served on a Design Team that was empowered to identify training needs and to work out the nuts and bolts of procedures that would enable the teams. They continued to hold a series of off-site meetings that not only kept people informed but also required people to make decisions that would affect the nature of this move toward SDWTs. They promised jobs to all the supervisors and other salaried employees who were to be displaced by this move to SDWTs. Then they asked these same employees to write their own job descriptions and performance review standards in a manner that would enable them to add value to the production process in their half of the plant. They did many things to prepare the organization and the people for this application of the team concept.

They felt they achieved some successes. Some groups took the horse by the reins and learned to work together in quality fashion. A few took advantage of the situation, and this upset many people. Some individually and some collectively slacked off from work and didn't meet production goals or make the decisions needed to solve some problems. However, most just felt they had no idea what was expected of them. The leadership would respond by saying they wanted the people to decide because they were in the best position to know what needed to get done. The people had been told what to do for years. They had occasionally been asked to react to plans and problems and come up with solutions, but they had never been given such license to design their own work system. The experiment began to flounder. People from the top to the bottom of this organization seemed to be making genuine efforts, but they didn't know where they were really headed.

Finally, it was suggested that each team might have different needs. Each team had to assess its own level of development and identify their own strengths and weaknesses. They had gotten so deeply into thinking about the large system change the team concept experiment was to carry that they forgot to look at the individual pieces. The assessments revealed that a few problems were shared by all of the teams, but others by only a few, and every team had some unique issues to work through.

A key problem for all of the teams was a lack of clear goals. The message during the launch activities seemed to indicate that the "goal" was to generate teams and launch a new product. Much information was being shared regarding the steps and decisions made by the various teams and what the overall production records were, but the individual teams did not really know if they were performing effectively. The data-gathering system produced information too late, and the information wasn't shared with the individual teams. Each team had differing needs, but the one problem that virtually every team had was that they were not really able to assess whether they were performing well on a day-to-day basis. Thus, they had a general sense of direction but did not receive specific data to know if the team was progressing toward the goal.

A task force was assembled to tackle the data-gathering problem. Management took responsibility for figuring out production standards at a more microlevel. The union did its best to ensure that the teams would have equitable work loads based on the input of hourly group leaders. Once specific goals were established that were performance related, attainable, and measurable, confidence in the team concept was renewed and "hard data" became available to verify the success of the process.

During the assessment, some teams admitted that when they had been given the opportunity to form their own departmental teams, they chose to work with friends without thinking through the range of talents needed to get the jobs done. They also realized that much of the early training they had received focused on relationships. They had fun at these sessions and found them interesting, but they were now left with goals they couldn't really fulfill. They inventoried the talent on the team using exercise 7, "Discovering the Talent on Your Team" (found in chapter 5), and identified members in other parts of the organization who had the skills they were missing. They sought the help of these people on a part-time basis and as trainers. They then dedicated more of their allotted training time to developing the technical skills needed to fulfill their responsibilities.

Many group leaders reported confusion over their new roles. Although the previous supervisors retained employment, some of them were reluctant to help the hourly group leaders through the transition. A three-level role clarification meeting was held off site. Upper management tried to help the "displaced" supervisors and area managers identify new prescribed and discretionary responsibilities using a modification of the Job Expectation Technique (found in chapter 6). In turn, the same process was used to clarify the roles and responsibilities of the hourly group leaders. This effort was only moderately successful at first. Across time, those managers and leaders who had formed more constructive interpersonal relations continued to work on achieving clarity. However, some parts of the plant, and, thus, the teams in those areas, continue to suffer from this problem.

During the assessment, it became clear that some teams were having problems with their meetings. Some meetings seemed to be strictly social gatherings and others became bitch-and-gripe sessions. Some were dominated by a few vocal members and others were forums in which members passively waited for the hourly group leader to tell them what to do. These teams were asked to apply the 4-A problem-solving model (see chapter 7) to improve their meetings. They brainstormed all the problems they were having with the sessions, analyzed the causes of these problems, generated creative solutions to the chief causes, and then identified a specific action plan to implement the best solutions they could devise. The teams are continuing to monitor the effectiveness of their meetings using exercise 14, "Team Meeting Questionnaire" (found in chapter 7).

A few of the teams identified their chief weakness to be some "personality conflict." Perhaps the most interesting was the Design Team itself. Three strongly Introverted Thinking type males came across as aloof to some of the Extraverted Feeling type members. The *Myers-Briggs Type Indicator* (MBTI; described in chapter 8), was used to help each member examine his or her personal style. Through a series of exercises, people began to see how these various styles helped as well as hindered the team's efforts to work together. What originally appeared to be judgmental attitudes turned out to be merely differences in how some reserved and cautious members approached the proposed change effort. The more the members viewed the dynamic as a difference in style rather than a personal judgment, the more the group reported progress on addressing their problem.

The Design Team combined this attempt to improve interpersonal relations with a need to gain more reinforcement for working in a team-oriented manner. The team utilized exercise 20,

"Contributing to the Work Group" (described in chapter 9) and ensured that each teammate received feedback regarding how she or he contributed to the work of this group. This allowed the group to celebrate diversity and recognize all the levels of risk taking that had taken place to move the organization down the path to self-directed work teams.

Two teams continue to dislike each other. The teams work in adjacent areas and spend much of their time blaming each other for anything that goes wrong. Both teams admit that this has become counterproductive. They have agreed to attend an off-site meeting to confront this conflict. They will use exercise 22, "Do As Well As You Can!" (found in chapter 10), which will confirm the conclusion that working together produces better numbers than competing with each other. There are some deep-seated resentments that primarily result from perceptions of work load inequity. In fact, it is clear that there are cliques within each team and the intergroup conflict actually involved rivalries between more than two teams. A variation of the Post Office Technique (found in chapter 10) will be used to begin the negotiations for changes in group behavior. Ultimately, a task force consisting of representatives from all the parties will be formed and asked to use the 4-A problem-solving model (from chapter 7) to systematically identify and resolve the myriad of concerns affecting the parties. The task force will report its recommendations at another joint meeting of the two departments and will be asked to continue to meet on an ongoing basis to resolve the remaining issues and prevent future conflicts.

This case study shows that even after a successful launch, a team concept idea can still run into problems. The Seven Key Components of Effective Teams described in chapters 4 through 10 has been proving to be useful in overcoming the problems of this site. The teams described in this case study are still working at it. They solve some problems and discover some others. Remember, team building is a process. Across time, they are verifying that they are better off than they were before they established teams. They have come to realize that they are out to achieve continuous improvement, not perfection. They are committed to use exercise 3, "Team Diagnostic Questionnaire" (contained in chapter 3) periodically to pinpoint what they need to work on next. They are taking teams seriously at this plant. The next seven chapters will provide you with the tools and exercises needed to help your teams travel down the same path.

CHAPTER 4

Clear Sense of Direction

Two or more individuals interacting with each other are considered a group. If a group has a purpose to accomplish, we call it a team. Thus, goals define the very reason for a team to exist. They provide a team with a purpose and a sense of direction. Perhaps no other component of team effectiveness is as important. In this chapter, we will examine why goals are so important to teams, why managers and team leaders often resist setting goals, approaches to setting goals that will gain the commitment of team members, strategies for using goal statements, and exercises that can be used with your teams to establish effective goals.

Why Goals Are Important to Teams

Goals provide a source of motivation by themselves. Why does having a goal motivate people to act? They focus the team on the direction we are heading. They allow individuals to compete against a standard rather than against fellow teammates. They establish a way of determining whether we have collectively succeeded. They focus on the future and they help provide meaning to our actions. Effective teams need clear goals.

Providing a Sense of Direction

Goals provide teams with a focus, a sense of direction. As figure 1 illustrates, if each individual in a group acted in a random manner, their actions would cancel each other out. Vector theory would predict that.

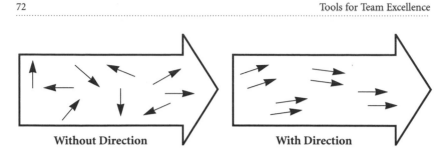

Figure 1 Team Members With and Without a Unified Sense of Direction

Goals act as a magnet, aligning the energy and actions of individuals. If the goals attract the individuals completely, the total force available on the team is maximized, as the figure also illustrates.

However, even if the goals realign each individual only a few degrees, the sum total of energy available to the team increases dramatically. Goals direct the attention of the members. It is hard to move forward unless the team looks toward where it is headed. Goals tell us where we are headed. Once a team knows where it is headed, it can participate in the development of effective work strategies. Exercise 5 provides a form that teammates can fill out at a meeting or a team training session. Each individual should take some time to fill out their responses to the questions privately. The group discussion of the answers will provide a good starting point for clarifying the team's sense of direction. A collective response to question 1 provides the team with a mission statement and question 2 provides a vision statement. Responses to questions 5 and 6 should lead to a planning session in which the team decides how to capitalize on the forces for and minimize the forces against achieving its vision.

Providing a Source of Motivation

Human beings have a general need to accomplish things. Some feel this need more strongly than others, but it is a need that everyone has. Have you ever watched a telethon for a charitable cause? When the host sets a concrete goal ("We need 10 calls in the next 5 minutes" or "Let's top last year's total of $2 million"), more viewers are motivated to act. In fact, as the tote board shows that the level of donations is approaching a goal, there is an increase in activity. Research by Edwin Locke and others verifies this pattern of behavior. Goals provide a target for people, and hitting a target provides them with satisfaction.

EXERCISE 5

Developing a Shared Sense of Direction

Directions: Have each individual privately respond to the following questions regarding his or her sense of the team's direction. Then develop a collective response to each question.

1. What do you believe is the major purpose for your team's existence?

2. Based on all you now know about teams, what is your vision of what your team should be like? Describe what your team would look like on a day-to-day basis if it were living up to its potential. How would it be different from what is in place now?

3. How many of your teammates share the same vision of your team's purpose and potential? How many teammates care enough to work together to make your team better?

4. How will you be able to tell if your team is getting better or getting worse over the next month or two?

5. What are the forces pushing you to become the vision of a team as you described it in question 2? What does your team and organization have going for it that leads you to believe that you might become that vision?

6. What are the forces, obstacles, barriers, pitfalls, and/or sources of resistance that might have to be overcome in order to become the vision of a team as you described it in question 2?

Channeling the Competitive Urge

Human beings also like to win, and winning involves competition. Individuals can compete with each other or they can compete against a goal. When individuals compete against each other, hurt feelings can often emerge. When individuals compete with each other, they withhold information from their competitors. When individuals lose a competition, they tend to either get even or withdraw. Do you want a team of people with hurt feelings who withhold information from each other and use the next project as a means to get even? Competition is a source of stimulation, and, if that stimulation is not too intense, performance levels will be enhanced. When team members want to accomplish a goal, they see the need to work together.

Goals funnel the competitive stimulus toward behaviors conducive to the desires of the organization and the needs of the individuals on the team. Goal statements attempt to channel the competitive urge but require a management style that directs individuals toward a sense of commitment to work together. Goals mobilize effort.

Establishing Mutual Accountability

Measures of progress toward the accomplishment of team goals verify whether the team is on target. If an organization is serious about using teams as its basic building blocks, accountability must be established at the group, not the individual, level. Knowing that the team is achieving its goals provides a source of pride. Concern about whether the team will achieve its goals can produce peer pressure. Using peer pressure can lead to all kinds of stress and abuses (e.g., violation of work rules) and is a source of negative reinforcement. Research by Skinner and others has verified that negative reinforcers motivate people to increase certain behaviors in order to avoid punishments. When a team is held accountable for accomplishing goals, individual team members might either fear receiving the scorn of their teammates for failing to carry an equitable share of the load or just not want to let down the people they care about. Without a clear statement of goals, the team will never really know if it is doing enough and whether it will be noticed by others. Research on *social loafing*, where a team member rides on the coattails of other team members, shows that when team members feel their efforts can't really be identified they exert little effort on behalf of the team (Price, 1987).

Making Sense of What the Team Is Doing

A task assigned to an individual on a team may not provide a whole, meaningful sense of accomplishment by itself. It may make sense only when the sum total of the tasks being performed as a team is apparent. The goal and how our tasks fit in order to accomplish the goal provides meaning to our work. Doing something meaningful is a core dimension of a satisfying job, as the research of Hackman and others has pointed out (Hackman and Oldham, 1976). The goals help us to see the forest from the trees. Certain personality types will find this to be more important than others. Still other people will need to strongly believe in the goal before it will have the desired effect on their behavior. This topic will be addressed more thoroughly in chapter 8. Thus, a goal that is merely a logical extension of the sum of a variety of tasks may not provide the full benefit for such people. In general, however, adults want to know why the things they are being asked to do make sense. Goal statements are an attempt to rationalize just that. When things make sense, people are more likely to provide persistent effort at working toward them.

Focusing on the Future

Discussion of past events can help clear the air and provide some lessons to be learned. In the short term, these discussions interrupt production–performance-related activities. Focusing on today provides activities that help us survive and get through the day, but it may not lead to the hope of achieving grander things. Goal statements articulate our hopes. Focusing on the future can help us to let go of the past. Focusing on the future can help us tolerate the frustrations of the present. A key to happiness for many is the belief that greater things are possible. A key to success is working to make these dreams come true. Thus, goal statements that focus a team on the future can help with everything from mundane problems such as interruptions caused by bickering about the past to inspirational opportunities to strive toward achieving the great things ahead.

Why Managers Often Resist Setting Clear Goals

If goal statements provide so many potential advantages to managing a team, why are so many supervisors reluctant to set clear goals? For one thing, when goals are set and announced, the manager will be held accountable for them. Ideally, the whole team will be held mutually accountable. However, the reality in most organizations today is that the manager of the team is the person who will be blamed by upper management if the goals are not reached. If the team has a series of losses, the manager (coach) loses his or her job or is at least made to feel the pressure of the failure. Since most organizations do not take teams seriously enough to establish mutual accountability, many managers practice a style of leadership known as CYA, or cover your behind. They ensure that they have a scapegoat, alternative explanations for the failure, and a means of verifying that they were doing what they were supposed to be doing. Since it is clear that a manager does not really have full control over all the things the team needs to accomplish, many will be reluctant to declare clear goals in advance. However, such actions can reduce a leader's credibility in the eyes of team members. It models the behavior of excuse making, a model readily imitated by others. This all leads to further erosion of belief in the team approach to getting things done.

Setting goals in advance also limits the post hoc explanations of what the team has accomplished during a given time period. Since the future is not truly predictable anyway, many managers would rather "see what happens" and then build a case for why those results and activities constituted the appropriate things to do after the fact. Accomplishing or even exceeding targets of performance established in advance would be the ideal thing to do, but it is far easier to find flaws in performance. Why set up this potential for grief in advance when you can just wait and justify what happened without having to compare that to an established goal? Still others fear that if the team is able to accomplish its goals this time, it only sets up the expectation of doing even more in a future situation. This concern over accelerating expectations (and the potential for manipulation and exploitation) is shared by team members as well as the team's manager.

Managers also resist goal setting in advance because it is difficult to do well. The goal may be very difficult to state in measurable terms. The organization may have inadequate systems to capture the data needed to measure whether the goals were truly accomplished. The culture of the organization may be biased against documenting the facts, or it may be felt that such activities will be seen as supporting a culture that discourages trust. Finally, many managers do not know how to set goals that are appropriate and motivating. They may not be given access to the necessary organizational data or may not have been trained to recognize the characteristics of well-stated goals.

How to Set Team Goals

Some managers simply do not know how to develop clear goal statements. Training sessions on the topic are rarely provided. The following basic principles and steps can help managers, team leaders, and team members fulfill the essential task of establishing a clear sense of direction with well written goal statements.

Establish the Purpose of the Team First

Before setting performance targets, a team needs to know why it exists. Thus, the organization needs to know what the team's goals and strategies are first. Then, within the context of what the organization is trying to accomplish, team members deserve to know what role they will collectively play. How do we fit in the game plan? Adults learn more, work harder, and receive more satisfaction from activities that they find meaningful. As children, we were all asked to engage in work at school and at home. We primarily did the work because some authority figure (e.g., parent, teacher) said, "because I told you to do it." Some organizations and managers attempt to treat their workforces in the same way. If the authority figure is strong enough, they may gain compliance, but they won't gain commitment. Human beings don't commit to things that don't mean much to them. Understanding why a team exists and how it is being asked to help the organization achieve its purpose provides a basis to perform meaningful work.

Provide Teams With the MAPS They Need

Statements of team goals should satisfy four criteria:

- Measurable
- Attainable
- Performance related
- Specific

By *measurable*, it is meant that the statement makes it easy to document whether the goal was actually accomplished or not. The statement needs to specify how much must be accomplished up to what standard and by when. Examples include "The team will produce 1,000 parts of a size that is within .001 of the specifications provided by our customers each work day over the next thirty days"; "Our faculty will publish no less than one article per faculty member in the journals listed in our evaluation document each academic year"; and "Our complaint department will respond to every customer inquiry within twenty-four hours and provide a determination regarding the complaint within ten working days in a manner whereby no less than 80 percent of the complaining customers say they are 'completely satisfied with the determination' and 99 percent of the complaining customers say they are 'more satisfied than not satisfied with the determination' on the survey administered to complaining customers every month."

The ideal way of making something measurable is to quantify it. However, some goals may defy quantification. Some goals will be of the nature of "Did you do it or didn't you do it?" The goals must be stated in terms such that ambiguity is eliminated. There should be a clear means of documenting and monitoring accomplishments and/or progress.

Goals that are impossible to reach will frustrate, not motivate, people. Ideally, the goals will be challenging but *attainable.* They will require team members to attend to their behaviors and deliver their skills, resulting in the satisfaction of achievement. Goals clarify expected levels of performance and effort. Goals that are set too low will not have the same effect, according to the research of McClelland and others. A few have argued that goals should be purposely set at a level that is impossibly high. They suggest that any goal statement sets up a ceiling that the team will believe it cannot or should not break through. They believe that setting impossibly high goals will result in higher levels of performance as people put out their full effort, even when they fall short. A manager might get a group to try this system once or twice, but when people are not really held accountable for not achieving a goal, credibility will suffer. The group will discount, in their minds, what the "real" goal is, for example, He is asking for 200, he must really need 150. Many people will not even try to achieve a goal that is set impossibly high. They may think, Why bother if we can't achieve it anyway.

Setting a goal that is challenging but attainable, one that is neither too low nor too high, requires knowledge of the capabilities of the people and systems involved. Thus, time and learning from experience is needed. A manager or team leader who wants to build an effective team needs to let the members know that goal setting is something that is to be continuously improved on. In addition, the leader may want to have the team participate in the goal-setting process. Research indicates that the average team will set goals at a higher level than the average manager will. Collaborative goal setting establishes ownership. Team members will be more dedicated to accomplishing goals that they helped establish than they will be to goals that are imposed on them. The exception to this rule may be the case of a new team. If the team is inexperienced with the task of setting goals and the team members have not had time to establish how they will work together on tasks, they will be at a loss as to how high the goals should be set. Research by Hersey and Blanchard (1977) indicates that under such circumstances, the experienced manager should establish the goal and explain why it is appropriate. If the team is very inexperienced, the manager may even need to tell the team members exactly how they need to work together to accomplish the goals. Across time, the manager, or leader, should adjust his or her style to allow for a more participative approach. Whether the team is experienced or whether the goals are set by the leader or collaboratively by the team, the team needs measurable and attainable goals.

Goal statements must also be *performance related.* The goals must be seen by team members as appropriate and must make sense in light of the team's purpose. If a person is on a sales staff and is told that the team's goal is to make the customer satisfied even to the point where their actions would make profitability impossible, members might not respect the goal. If the goal of the team is stated as "To communicate with each other more frequently," they may like the idea, but unless they see a direct link between frequency of communication and high performance, they won't take the team approach to work seriously. Members may instead believe, They just want us to be more complacent, and if things are going okay, we can talk to each other, but if profits decline, they will tell us to "Shut up and get to work." It is imperative that the goals are clearly consistent with the reason this team exists and how it supports the profitability and other goals of the larger organization. If teams are used to promote sociability, they will be seen as second-class structures rather than a primary strategy for organizational effectiveness. Team goals should reflect the dual purposes of the team approach—accomplishing more/better work, and promoting the quality of the work lives of the people getting the work done. If the goal statement fails to be performance related, it indicates that someone is not taking teams seriously as a business strategy.

Finally, and most importantly, goals must be stated in very *specific* terms. Research by Locke and Latham (1990) confirms that the more specific the goal is, the more likely it will motivate people to work toward it. The more specific the goals are, the more focused the team will be. The goal statement should clearly identify the quantity and quality standards to be reached. Feedback regarding whether these standards are being met provides a team with the sense of direction so crucial for team effectiveness. The team needs to know: Are we getting better or getting worse? Goal statements that are Measurable, Attainable, Performance related and Specific provide the MAPS needed for the journey towards excellence.

How to "Use" Goal Setting
as a Team-Building Strategy

Performance is a function of ability, motivation, and opportunity. The very act of setting goals is an opportunity for teams to set the stage for better performance. As stated earlier, goals are a source of motivation. Team members and leaders must have the knowledge and skills (abilities) to set goals appropriately. Thus, team meetings dedicated to goal setting are team-building and performance enhancement activities. Let's examine why.

Participation in Goal Setting as an Educational Strategy

Most companies have treated the goal-setting process as a management prerogative. This, combined with the fact that jobs are usually defined narrowly rather than broadly, leads most team members to think of goals as somebody else's directive. Goal statements that satisfy the criteria outlined in the previous section can still be a source of motivation, even if lower-level employees are not involved in the goal-setting process; however, their involvement can produce two benefits: (1) It educates people on the broader organizational realities facing the company and provides a perspective for how the team needs to work in order to contribute to the organization's success, and (2) it can provide a sense of ownership of the goals that translates into committed rather than compliant behavior. Although it may take more time to set the goals by including team members in the process, management won't have to spend time explaining and selling the goals to the team that has to implement them. Participation clarifies expectations, and groups need that to coordinate the actions and perspectives of their members (Steiner, 1972). Instead of *talking* about providing training and opportunities to learn, the team will be *doing* it through a participative goal-setting session. Active learning is much more appealing to adults. A team fully educated in the options and which has helped select the targets to be accomplished is an asset to an organization.

Using Goals as the Basis for Decision Making

Once the team's goals have been set, it is crucial that they don't merely become ideals or words on a page. Decisions regarding issues such as procedures, assignments, and resource allocations should literally be justified in light of the goal statements. This produces several benefits, including frequent reminders of just what it is the team is supposed to be accomplishing, demonstrations of "walking the talk," and ongoing efforts to build and maintain trust. When determining production schedules, a systematic analysis should be made of how the schedule will lead to fulfillment of the team's goals. When allocating resources from a given budget, it should be verified that money is being spent in rough proportion to the priorities as they are outlined in the goal statements.

Using Goals to Identify Opportunities to Reinforce Team-Oriented Behaviors

Behaviors that are positively reinforced are more likely to be repeated. Team-oriented actions should not be taken for granted. Do not wait for extraordinary achievements before providing recognition and rewards for actions that result in accomplishment of goals stated in advance. The team needs to be recognized and individuals need to be rewarded for contributing to the team's success. This further aligns a group of individuals toward a common target without eliminating some natural feelings of self-interest. When an individual clearly sees that working for the team's goals results in personal needs being satisfied, she or he is more motivated to be a team player. The goal statements should be kept very visible and explanations should be given regarding how a reward is tied to the accomplishment of these goals. This issue will be explored in more detail in chapter 9.

Team-Building Activities for Goal Setting

Perhaps the ideal way to set goals as a team is to do it as part of a strategic planning session. This should not be an exercise for the sake of doing an exercise; it must be real. A team should not be invited to participate in a strategic planning session unless there is an intention to follow through on the plans produced. Too often, teams attend "retreats" and become enthused and refreshed by an active interchange of ideas, only to return to work and find that nothing has changed. While there are many preparations that must be undertaken for strategic planning sessions (e.g., choosing a site for the session, compiling data for the analyses, clarifying the boundaries within which the team must operate, establishing a systematic agenda to guide the

Table 7 The Five Steps of Strategic Planning

1. **Review your past: "What day is it?"**

   Study your organization's vision/mission statement (clearly identify *why* your team exists in light of this statement).

   Identify the key milestones your team has accomplished over the last one to five years (the highlights and lowlights).

   Describe what has happened in the organization and what decisions have affected your team over the last one to five years.

2. **Assess the current state of your team.**

   Report the data and anecdotal evidence regarding the "multiple bottom lines" your team dealt with.

   Assess your team's outcomes.

   Assess processes your team used to achieve those outcomes.

   Summarize the assessment of your team with a SWOT (strengths, weaknesses, opportunities, threats) statement.

3. **Identify goals that would represent successful resolution to your current problems.**

   Exercise awareness: Which problems deserve attention?

   Exercise analysis: What are the chief causes of the problems?

   Consider alternatives: What could be done differently?

   Plan action: Who should do what with whom by when and how?

4. **Envision the direction and new elements of your future.**

   Identify likely future demands that your team may have to respond to.

   Picture your ideal/preferred future: What would this team be accomplishing if it were fully living up to its potential?

   Brainstorm new features/directions for your team.

   Envision the milestones you would achieve.

5. **Plan the actions/tactics needed for implementation.**

   Identify the forces for and against a new and improved team.

   Identify the strategies to capitalize on the forces for the team.

   Identify the strategies to reduce the forces against the team.

   Identify the steps that must be taken to implement the plan.

   Identify who is responsible for which elements of the plan.

   Identify a time line for achieving the elements of the plan.

---

discussions), time blocks should be reserved subsequent to the planning session to follow up on the ideas the team is expected to identify. Table 7 provides a five-step process for teams to follow when developing a strategic plan: reviewing, assessing, problem solving, envisioning the future, and action planning.

EXERCISE 6

Individual Action Planning

Directions: Respond to the following questions regarding your team's goals.

1. What am I to specifically accomplish that would contribute to the team's ability to accomplish its overall goals?
2. How will I know if I have accomplished my goals? What will be measured to verify this?
3. How will I go about accomplishing my goals?
4. Whose help will I need to follow through on this promise?
5. Why do I want to meet these goals?

It is important that every goal identified by the team be stated in a manner that satisfies the criteria of being Measurable, Attainable, Performance related, and Specific. Thus, the goals provide the team with the MAPS they need to succeed.

Zander (1980) points out that there are really four types of group goals: (1) each member's goals for the group, (2) each member's goals for him or herself, (3) the group's goals for the member, and (4) the group's overall goals for itself. This chapter has focused on the fourth type of goal, and the MAPS criteria helps document each group goal statement. In order to track the individual goals represented by the first three types of goals identified by Zander, exercise 6, "Individual Action Planning," should be completed by each member and shared with the team. Then, at the next team meeting, members can share what progress they believe they made and teammates can provide feedback on what they observed.

Summary

What could be more important than clarifying a team's goals? How can we ever expect a team to be successful if we don't define what success will look like? Goals provide a sense of direction and they provide a team with a sense of purpose. Goals pull teams together, yet most teams operate with vague notions of what their targets should be. Individuals are given assignments and are grouped together into departments or work sections. But if they are going to develop effective teams, organizations must insist on goal statements for each team that are measurable, attainable, performance related, and specific. Research shows that teams that had such goal statements performed at a level one standard deviation higher than groups without such goals (O'Leary-Kelly, Martocchio, and Frink, 1994). Teams must be given a chance to succeed. They must be given the time and access to information, and the team must be pulled together to make it clear what the team's goals are. This first component of effective teams, establishing goals, will set the stage for future success.

CHAPTER 5

Talented Members

Performance is a function of abilities, motivation, and opportunities. There are playground basketball teams where the guys know the goals of the game, could describe plays to run, and get along well with each other; but if they don't have the talent to dribble, pass, shoot, and defend, well, they won't win many games. That is true for the performance of a sports team or a work team. If you have a team of engineers who can't design well or solve the technical problems associated with the product you want to make, you will not have a successful engineering team. Although most published models of team effectiveness don't mention the need for talent directly, it is an obvious crucial component. Hollywood portrayals of teams often glorify mediocre teams (e.g., *The Bad News Bears* or *The Mighty Ducks*) rising to the top while vilifying top-rated teams as egotists. But even these movies show team players (often children) discovering and developing their talents. For a team to be effective, the necessary talent must be there, and it has to be utilized and continually developed and improved.

Talent Must Exist

When a team is formed, someone must have enough vision regarding what the team is supposed to accomplish so that the full range of competencies needed can be identified. Selection procedures need to be valid enough to assess whether candidates can do the job. This may mean concentrating more on skills and less on personality traits.

Leadership styles can be adjusted to motivate people to work harder or smarter, but people can't deliver what they don't have. Ideally, the technical skills and knowledge required to do the job should be determined through job analysis techniques and candidates should be expected to demonstrate their abilities to fulfill these requirements before being placed on a team. This may include some basic skills such as reading, writing, and computational math. Some abilities will be difficult to assess. Letters of recommendation and interviews with candidates are commonly used to attempt to make such decisions. Unfortunately, many people responsible for such selection decisions are not systematic in their screening procedures, tend to pick people they feel comfortable with, and are quick to form an impression of the candidate. If we are going to take teams seriously, managers and human resource specialists must be trained on how to administer tests, conduct interviews, and make observations, all in nondiscriminatory ways.

Most high-involvement, team-oriented plants (e.g., the original Saturn plant) expect more than technical skills from their employees. They want to ensure that employees have the knowledge and skills needed to work on a team. They assess candidates on such things as communication skills, ability to facilitate consensus decisions in group settings, problem solving, and planning skills. Candidates are expected to participate in a series of small-group exercises while trained assessors observe who displays team-oriented behaviors and to what degree. Some plants have allowed existing team members to make these assessments when adding new members. The team members are expected to interview and observe candidates who have been prescreened to ensure that they already have the needed technical skills.

Talent Must Be Utilized

Once team members have worked together for a while, there is a natural tendency to make assumptions regarding each person's range of talent as a function of his or her job title. We may, for example, assume that secretaries are idea executors, not idea generators. We may likewise assume that librarians wouldn't make good spokespersons. By doing so, we fail to continue to search out the hidden talents that exist in virtually all of us. On the other side of the coin, many of us would feel inhibited to proclaim our talents to others. I have found it useful to have teams periodically dedicate meetings to become reacquainted with each other. In exercise 7, "Discovering the Talent on Your Team," I get teammates to act as "the designated bragger" for each other. If you attempt to produce a list of all the collective talents of the team as indicated in the "introductions" generated through this exercise, you are likely to be left with the feeling that you are on a powerful team capable of delivering a great deal of talent for the good of the organization. Begin the session with a discussion of three questions: (1) Why should we inventory the talent of this team? (2) What inhibits people from letting teammates know what their knowledge, talents, and qualities are? and (3) What can we do to encourage each individual to clearly state his or her strengths? Then follow this process with exercise 7.

If we are going to achieve team excellence, we need people to be peak performers. Charles Garfield (1986) conducted research on some of the world's greatest athletes and also on people who were extraordinarily successful in business. He found that peak performers are not much different from ordinary people. Teams can get extraordinary results from ordinary people when each member is (1) truly focused on the mission she or he is to accomplish for the team, (2) capable of feeling truly relaxed and focused at the same time, (3) willing to mentally rehearse actions and statements she or he is going to make beforehand, and (4) willing to let go of the past and excessive self-monitoring and allow his or her inner self to perform. Exercise 8 provides a list of questions you can utilize to assess your own readiness to be a peak performer.

Talent Must Be Continually Developed

Being committed to a team not only means believing in the team's goals, it also means dedicating the necessary time to update the knowledge and skills your team needs you to deliver. In sports, rookies mature and grow from their experiences. In sports, players learn new pitches, perfect jump shots, and are expected to continue to practice even the basics of their trade. Just because you were a very competent accountant when you were selected to join a team does not

EXERCISE 7

Discovering the Talent on Your Team

Directions: Follow the instructions below and then answer the questions as directed or perform the activity to discover the talent —hidden and otherwise—on your team.

1. **Develop three lists:**
   - What are the key skills, knowledge, and qualities that I bring to this team that are directly related to the performance of my job assignments?
   - What are the key skills, knowledge, and qualities that I bring to this team that help this group of individuals function as a team?
   - What are the "hidden" skills, knowledge, and qualities that I have that I don't think everyone on this team knows about?

2. **Now pair up with a "designated bragger" who will:**
   - Listen to your lists and ask clarifying questions.
   - Add to your lists talents she or he has perceived that you might not have thought of yourself.
   - Ask probing questions so that the two of you together can come up with other items to add to your lists.

3. **Switch roles with your designated bragger and repeat activity 2.**

4. **Each designated bragger should deliver a great "introduction" of his or her partner in this exercise.**

5. **A running inventory should be recorded to capture the collective talents of this team.**

6. **Discuss the inventory as a team in three ways:**
   - What does the inventory tell us about this team?
   - To what extent is the talent of this team being utilized?
   - What talents, knowledge bases, and qualities are we missing?

mean you will always be on top of the latest tax laws and accounting procedures. Just because you knew a given machine does not mean you will always be on the cutting edge of the technology related to your assignment. When teammates see peers dedicating time to practice, develop, and advance their skills, commitment to high-performance

EXERCISE 8

The Key Skills and Qualities of Peak Performers

Directions: For all items, circle the rating that is most accurate for the situation described, with 0 = not at all, 1 = a little bit, 2 = somewhat, 3 = to a large extent, and 4 = very much.

1. To what extent can you clearly articulate your personal mission?

   0   1   2   3   4

2. To what extent are you committed to the achievement of your personal mission?

   0   1   2   3   4

3. To what extent are you committed to learn from your efforts to achieve your personal mission?

   0   1   2   3   4

4. To what extent do you set clear goals for yourself?

   0   1   2   3   4

5. To what extent are you flexible regarding how your goals are to be reached?

   0   1   2   3   4

6. To what extent do you manage your time well?

   0   1   2   3   4

7. To what extent have you found ways to be assigned to activities that are directly related to the accomplishment of your personal mission?

   0   1   2   3   4

8. To what extent are you good at organizing groups of people to accomplish tasks relevant to your mission?

   0   1   2   3   4

9. To what extent are you good at setting up systems or procedures to ensure that things get done and continue to get done?

   0   1   2   3   4

10. To what extent do you prioritize well?

   0   1   2   3   4

EXERCISE 8 continued

11. To what extent are you an effective problem solver?

    0   1   2   3   4

12. To what extent are you a calculative risk taker?

    0   1   2   3   4

13. To what extent do you weigh the pros and cons of options before making decisions?

    0   1   2   3   4

14. To what extent do you avoid the paralysis of analysis?

    0   1   2   3   4

15. To what extent do you empower others, that is, interact with others in a manner that helps make them feel more capable?

    0   1   2   3   4

16. To what extent do you provide praise to others for their actions and efforts?

    0   1   2   3   4

17. To what extent do you manage stress well?

    0   1   2   3   4

18. To what extent can you mentally visualize actions (rehearse them mentally) before you take them?

    0   1   2   3   4

19. To what extent can you delegate assignments in a manner that helps the person understand the benefits of taking on the assignment?

    0   1   2   3   4

20. To what extent are you a perfectionist?

    0   1   2   3   4

21. To what extent are you keeping yourself fit and healthy?

    0   1   2   3   4

22. To what extent are you maintaining better than average relationships with family and friends?

    0   1   2   3   4

standards is likely to occur. Some employee involvement efforts have taken continuous improvement as a theme that problem-solving teams are expected to believe in. Continuous improvement, or *kaizan,* as it is known in Japan, is typically applied as a philosophy of improving products and processes. It should also be applied to people.

Summary

While motivational techniques and systematic planning can help a team deliver to the best of its abilities, it will never be fully effective unless the members have the talent needed to perform their jobs well. The full range of competencies needed to accomplish the tasks must be available to a team. The talents of the members must be identified and utilized. If certain knowledge or skill bases are missing, additions to the team may need to be recruited on a full- or part-time basis. Training offers another strategy for teams to add to their pool of talent. Team members must be willing to continue to hone their skills and advance their knowledge. Teams are taken seriously when the knowledge, skills, and abilities exist and are activated. It is only then that a long-term success story is possible with teams. It is then that team excellence can be achieved.

CHAPTER 6

Clear and Enticing Responsibilities

B asketball teams typically play with two guards, and such players need to know whether the team expects them to play the role of a shooting guard or a point guard. Both kinds of guards shoot the ball, dribble, make passes, and play defense. However, the point guard acts as the quarterback of the team when they are on offense. Point guards are responsible for setting up the plays and primarily for passing the ball to an open teammate and only occasionally taking shots themselves. Fulfilling the role contributes to the team's ability to accomplish its goals through strategies designed in advance. The differing talents of the guards help determine which players should take on which roles.

Once a work team knows what it is to accomplish, the various tasks needed to succeed can be identified through job analysis techniques. These tasks can be used to define the roles of team members. The roles can be assigned if the talent of the members is already known or, if it is a new team about to be formed, the job analysis can be used to identify the criteria for selecting team members. The more clearly the role is defined, the better the member will be able to focus his or her talent. However, if the role is too narrowly defined, the team may lose out on the opportunity to capitalize on the multiple talents of that member. The key is getting enough clarity to know how to contribute to the team's success while providing each member with a sense of individual accomplishment and satisfaction. When a team has the right mix of tasks that are well differentiated and integrated, members have the sense that none of us succeed unless we all succeed.

Specialized Roles

There are advantages and disadvantages to clearly defining exactly what is expected from each individual on a team. The clearer one's role is, the more specialized it becomes. Specialization provides the opportunity for mastery of a task, since one is expected to do it again and again. With mastery comes efficiency, expertise, and effectiveness. Teammates know who to turn to for information relevant to the tasks of each role. Clearly defined roles help make selection, training, and performance appraisal more objective. This establishes who is accountable for what. Vroom's theory of motivation points out that the first step in motivating employees is to help them clearly perceive that whatever is expected of them is possible. When roles are ambiguous, uncertainty regarding whether one is capable of doing the right thing prevails.

However, roles can be overdefined. Job descriptions can become legalistic documents encouraging each person to only care about his or her assignments. When a situation calls for help, one is then tempted to say, "It's not my job." Specialized job assignments work well in simple, predictable, routine situations that call for speed. Job specialization was the norm in manufacturing during the first half of the twentieth century. The "classical school of management," as exemplified in *Scientific Management* by F. W. Taylor and *The Ideal Bureaucracy* by Max Weber, recommended it. Organizations were encouraged to separate the tasks of doing the work from planning or even inspecting the work. Taylor suggested that workers were as dumb as oxen and that management should identify the best way to do things and use money and fear of job loss as motivators to get workers to do what they are told. Work teams did not really consist of a number of independent players. Work teams had one person doing the thinking and the other players complying with that person's orders. Jobs in many industries became narrowly defined in that workers could fulfill their tasks without really thinking while getting paid a considerable amount of money.

Enriched Jobs

If the team is expected to deal with changes on a frequent basis, role definitions must be kept loose. The world changed during the 1960s and beyond. Organizations found themselves dealing with competition from all over the world. Consumers became more demanding.

Workers, who had plenty of brain power to contribute all along, also had more educational credentials and many made it clear that they desired to have more influence over decisions that affected their work lives. The very rate of change itself accelerated. Organizations started recognizing more of the benefits of getting employees involved in identifying and resolving organizational problems. At first, efforts to redesign jobs to make them more enriching experiences were made on a case-by-case basis. However, every time one job was "enriched" there were spin-off effects. Either supervisors felt threatened because their decision-making power became eroded, or other workers demanded to be treated with the same respect and dignity they saw the holders of enriched jobs receiving. Organizations found that the structure of teams provided a way to channel that input and give groups of employees a complete natural unit of work to identify with. In some organizations, teams began to be taken more seriously.

Task–Role Clarification Techniques

Between the job enrichment movement, the flattening of the organizational hierarchies, improvements in technology, and the increased capabilities of the average worker, members of work teams today are expected to fulfill many task roles. Does this mean everyone should just do everything? This would likely lead to chaos and fail to capitalize on the diverse talents potentially available on a given team. We still need all of our basketball guards to dribble, pass, and shoot, but we can improve our use of these talents by setting priorities through efforts to define the roles and responsibilities of each member of a team. This clarification as a team is essential. One approach to achieve this clarification is known as the *Job Expectations Technique* (JET), described below.

Job Expectations Technique (JET)

Before you begin to use this approach, make sure that everyone understands the goals of the organization and the goals of this team/group vis-à-vis the organization. Teams often utilize a consultant whose role in all this is to help with the original diagnosis, educate people on the steps of the JET process, and then facilitate the sessions without deciding who is right or wrong on issues. The technique is used as follows.

First, a diagnosis of the situation is conducted to verify that a role-clarification problem exists and whether the people with power are willing to use an interactive technique to resolve the problems. A strong commitment is needed to utilize this technique, with the knowledge that it may mean spending two to three hours per role in the group/team. Ideally, the role-clarification session is held off site and each team/group member is given the time needed to prepare for the session. One member at a time then presents what she or he sees as the prescribed and discretionary roles of his or her job. It is usually recommended that the manager of the team goes first and sets a standard for doing this thoroughly and nondefensively. Team members then react to each presentation by confirming what they agree with and offering different perspectives regarding what the prescribed and discretionary responsibilities should be. While this feedback is being offered, the presenter is to record all comments on a flip chart for later consideration. At the next session, all members re-present their roles, emphasizing how they incorporated the feedback of their teammates. Negotiations take place until a consensus is reached. Then each person must write up a job description for him or herself that accurately reflects the consensus. Periodic review and evaluation sessions should be held to verify whether people are fulfilling their roles and whether possible adjustments need to be made to the descriptions of those roles.

In addition to the task roles each member performs, certain team relations roles (a.k.a. social roles) must be fulfilled in order for a group of individuals to work effectively together. Exercise 9 describes another technique to assist a team identifying the needed task and relationship roles, as well as certain roles that team members may be portraying that interfere with the team's functioning. It consists of three forms—one each for the task, team relations, and "dysfunctional" roles—that each individual fills out and shares with the rest of the team. The fourth form is used to record feedback each member receives regarding changes in their roles on the team.

The Role of Leader

One of the more interesting sets of responsibilities a team needs to clarify is that of leadership. Teams need a sense of direction. This sense of direction unifies the diverse members of the team. This

EXERCISE 9

Clarifying the Task, Social, and Dysfunctional Roles on Your Team

Directions: For each of the four steps below, complete the activities as instructed.

Step 1: Analysis of the job tasks of our team

On this first form, list each job task that must be performed in order to do the work of your unit. Be specific. Some job classifications involve many smaller component tasks. Use additional sheets of paper as needed. After each task that you list, put the names or initials of the team members responsible for that piece of the work. If the task is something that is rotated among members, list the names of the members who perform the task and any recommendations regarding the schedule of rotation for that task in the column marked "Comments." Some tasks, for example, maintenance, may be performed by people who are not actually members of your team. Circle those items and comment on whether you believe the responsibility for the task should be restructured so that it is performed by a permanent member of your team.

Specific Job Task   **Person Responsible**   **Comments**

_____   _____   _____

_____   _____   _____

_____   _____   _____

_____   _____   _____

_____   _____   _____

_____   _____   _____

_____   _____   _____

_____   _____   _____

_____   _____   _____

_____   _____   _____

EXERCISE 9 continued

Step 2: Analysis of the team dynamic roles of our group

In order for a group of individuals to function as a team, members must find ways to interact beyond performing their job tasks. Some of these team dynamic roles help facilitate the tasks and some help build relationships between team members. Many of these roles are listed below. After each role, put the initials of the person (or persons) on your team who is most likely to perform that role for the team. Occasionally, everyone on the team may perform the role equally. In such cases, you may list "all." However, while some roles may be performed by everyone, it is clear that one or two people perform that role much more frequently than the other team members. In such cases, list only the people who perform the role more frequently.

Team Dynamic Roles	Person	Team Dynamic Roles	Person
Coordinator	_____	Opinion asker	_____
Opinion giver	_____	Goal setter	_____
Problem identifier	_____	Problem solver	_____
Meeting convener	_____	Information seeker	_____
Information giver	_____	Listener	_____
Feedback giver	_____	Praiser/Appreciator	_____
Conflict resolver	_____	Tension reliever	_____
Energizer/Encourager	_____	Standards setter	_____
Gatekeeper	_____	Decision pusher	_____
Progress monitor	_____	Risk taker	_____
Spokesperson	_____	Challenger	_____
Team celebrator	_____	Enforcer	_____
Procurer	_____	Initiator	_____
Group conscience	_____	Investigator	_____
Implementor	_____	Planner	_____
Volunteer	_____	Deadline setter	_____
Strategist	_____	Troubleshooter	_____

EXERCISE 9 continued

Step 3: Analysis of the dysfunctional roles of our team

Some team members may play roles that are disruptive to genuine efforts to improve team effectiveness and satisfaction. They might end up in these roles because they feel competitive with teammates or because they have their own agenda to satisfy. Everyone plays some of these roles occasionally. In small doses, these roles are harmless diversions. However, in larger doses, they reduce the team's ability to maximize performance and satisfaction. It isn't easy to constructively point out the impact the use of these roles has on a team. People become defensive, counter-attack, or make those brave enough to bring up these matters feel guilty. However, without a discussion of these roles and a commitment to avoid their use, a team will find it difficult to achieve excellence. Some of these roles are identified below. Put an "X" next to those roles that are likely to be played at least occasionally to the detriment of your team. This is a team effort, so you do not need to identify the individual likely to practice these dysfunctional roles. The purpose of this exercise is to draw attention to the impact of the role and to reduce the use of it within the group.

Dysfunctional Roles

Overuser of clowning   _____
Topic jumper   _____
Overuser of cynicism/sarcasm   _____
Overteller of "war" stories   _____
Nitpicker—finding the flaw   _____
Rejecter of ideas without reasons   _____
Blamer—who (not what) is at fault   _____
Excessive talker   _____
Credit taker for the team's work   _____
One-upmanship   _____
Back stabber   _____
User of team meetings for personal agenda   _____
"See, I told you so"   _____
Overuser of negativism—"Ain't it awful"   _____
Passive member—"Whatever you guys want"   _____
Silent member   _____
Dominator   _____
Manipulator   _____
Overanalyzer   _____
Overgeneralizer   _____

EXERCISE 9 continued

Premature decision maker   _____
Presenter of opinions as facts   _____
We–They thinker   _____
Status seeker   _____
Interrupter   _____
Apathetic soul   _____
Know-it-all   _____
Excuse maker   _____

Step 4: Role negotiations

Now that your team has discussed perceptions of the roles its members play, it's time to negotiate any changes needed to improve your team's effectiveness and satisfaction levels. Now each individual is to take a turn in "the hot seat." As a group, provide each individual constructive feedback on the following role issues:

1. The roles we see you currently fulfilling the best and want you to continue to fulfill are:

   _____

   _____

2. In order for our team to become more effective and satisfying, we would like you to fulfill the following roles more often:

   _____

   _____

3. In order for our team to become more effective and satisfying, we would like you to fulfill the following roles less often:

   _____

   _____

4. Now that you have heard our feedback, which role changes are you willing to commit to making on behalf of our team?

   _____

   _____

unity and cohesion can be achieved in several ways. Chapter 4 emphasized the need for clear goals to provide a sense of direction. United
action can also be achieved through focusing on a common enemy.
External conflict creates internal cohesion. A third way of uniting a
team is through the actions of an effective leader. In this section, we
will look at the role of management in an organization attempting to
institute a team concept and look at the variety of means to fulfill the
leadership role within teams.

Hundreds of research studies have attempted to identify just what
it takes to be an effective manager and leader. Originally, it was
thought that leadership was an inherited trait. We have all heard people express that a person appears to be a born leader. Actually, it is
more a matter that some people inherit more opportunities to practice
their leadership skills than others and some make use of those opportunities and some don't. In addition, other people make their own
opportunities. Perhaps more accurately, they establish or react to situations in a manner that influences other people. In fact, that is probably the best definition of leadership that can be offered: Leadership is
the attempt to influence. As Levinson and Rosenthal (1984) have written, "some leaders want to be leaders and see themselves as leaders.
Others rise to the occasion. In either case they see what has to be done
and do it." While some people may have a higher probability of succeeding at leadership than others, research has shown that adults can
learn to become effective leaders: "Wanting to lead and believing that
you can lead are only the departure points on the path to leadership.
Leadership is an art. . . . Ultimately, leadership development is a
process of self-development" (Kouzes and Posner, 1987).

Early writings regarding what it takes to be an effective manager are
referred to as the Classical School of Management Thought (Taylor,
Weber, Fayol, etc.). They declared that leadership should be delivered
by managers in an impersonal style. The emphasis was on the task,
and, as was pointed out earlier, the thought was that managers were
the ones with the brains needed to figure out what had to be done and
how best to do it. They suggested that there are four basic functions
managers must fulfill: planning, organizing, leading, and controlling.

The Human Relations Movement gained some credibility through
the Hawthorn Studies conducted in the 1920s and 1930s. Those
instrumental in the movement (Lewin, Lippitt, Likert, etc.) suggested that friendlier relations were called for. Managers became more

personable as they moved from an autocratic to a paternalistic style. Communications and concern for people were advocated. The slogan of "A happy worker is a productive worker" was even touted. As appealing as this slogan sounds, research and experience demonstrated that it was overly optimistic. There are happy workers who are not very productive, and some unhappy ones who are productive and feel that they have some great ideas on how things should be done at work but feel they haven't been given any say on these things.

Research studies conducted by faculty at Ohio State University and the University of Michigan in the next three decades became known as the Behavioral School of Management Thought. The results suggested that the classical and human relations schools each had half of the answer correct. The behaviorists concluded that effective managers/leaders must simultaneously be concerned with tasks and with people. They should initiate structure—define the subordinates' roles so that they know what is expected of them—and show consideration—express concern for subordinates' feelings and respect for their ideas. Blake and Mouton offered something called the *managerial grid* to help managers identify the degree to which they are "concerned for production" and "concerned for people." The ideal manager would have a high concern for both production and people, and would not attempt to compromise one at the expense of the other. A management style consistent with this would be conducive to building effective teams, since teams need a balance between task and relationship orientations.

In the 1970s and 1980s, some managers eventually moved toward a consultative style, that is, consulting with the workforce for their ideas but reserving decision-making authority for management. With the help of some brave union leaders, most notably Irving Bluestone and Don Ephlin of the United Auto Workers, workers were allowed to volunteer to be part of problem-solving teams that could make recommendations to management or to joint union–management steering committees. The emergence of quality of work life or employee involvement groups provided recognition that workers closest to the action have the intelligence and skills needed to help improve American business organizations. Over 80 percent of all Fortune 500 companies today claim to have some form of employee involvement as a basic process for running their businesses. The consultative style of leadership is conducive to the form of team concept that emphasizes shop floor problem-solving teams.

A few organizations eventually moved their management philosophies further by advocating a truly participative style of sharing leadership power and responsibility with teams of direct reports. Some established committees that could make *decisions,* not just *recommendations.* Others have moved toward real self-directed work teams, where hourly workers make the day-to-day decisions and the managers work with the rest of the organization to gain the support needed for the team to operate effectively and to help coordinate the actions of the various teams to ensure overall organizational effectiveness. Democratic principles such as free speech, the right to influence decisions affecting one's life, and even the opportunity to elect one's leaders can be seen in some of the organizations that have taken the steps to implement self-directed work teams. Incidentally, very few of those companies chose teams and democratic principles because it seemed like the right thing to do; they chose them because it is a practical thing to do and because it can make good business sense.

Having tracked the history of management thought from the classical school to self-directed work teams, what can we say about the four functions to be fulfilled by managers (i.e., planning, organizing, leading, and controlling)? As the times have changed, business organizations have increasingly seen the benefits of moving toward a more involving or participatory style of management. The functions of management haven't really changed, but the style of how to activate these functions has. Table 8 identifies the trends within each of the functions.

The style of management/leadership must change to support an implementation of any of the team concepts described in this book. In some organizations, it has been more than a change in an appointed leader's style. In some organizations, the role of leader has been incorporated into the team itself rather than as a function of management. This has been accomplished in at least two different ways: Sometimes a team leader is elected by the members of the team; other times, though less commonly, the leadership position is eliminated and the functions and roles originally fulfilled by a manager are now distributed among the remaining team members. Typically, an area manager is assigned to oversee several teams, providing coaching, expertise, and support. In any case, just which roles managers, leaders, and teams are expected to fulfill must be clarified. Henry Mintzberg conducted a series of famous studies in the 1970s to clarify just what a manager actually does. He concluded that the managerial job contains ten roles that can be categorized into three "families" of roles—

Table 8 The Transition From a Traditional to a Team-Oriented Manager

Planning

Traditional	Team oriented
Crisis management	Strategic planning
Satisfactory	High-performance goals
Quantity	Quantity and quality
Short term	Long term
One bottom line	Multiple bottom lines
Task	Task and relationship
Internal concerns	Internal and external (customer)

Organizing

Traditional	Team oriented
Tell/Sell	Develop together from start
Specialization	Cross-training and job rotation
My schedule	Our schedule
Secrecy	Frequent meetings, open sharing, and problem solving
Divide and conquer	Teamwork
Stability	Change and flexibility

Leading

Traditional	Team oriented
Gaining compliance	Building commitment
Hero	Developer
Inspiration for motivation	Role model
Autocratic (in charge)	Participative facilitator
Paternalistic	Consultative
Dictates	Structures
Training (teacher)	Learning partner
Answer giver	Question asker/supporter

Controlling

Traditional	Team oriented
Inspection	Self-observation
Monitor team	Monitor organization customer
Police	Self-discipline (peer pressure)
Blaming	Problem solving
Need to know	Openness
Chain of command	Customer relations
Training	Certifying competency
One performance evaluator	Multiple input
Individual reward	Team/Organization rewards
Monetary reward only	Money + recognition

interpersonal, informational, and decisional. Table 9 provides a description of Mintzberg's managerial roles system.

To clarify who will be responsible to fulfill each of these roles, the first step of the Job Expectations Technique described earlier in this chapter can be repeated. A version of this is popularly known as a Responsibility Chart or a Responsibility Matrix. It is used in many organizations attempting to plan for the transition of the leader's role under a team concept. The team, with the help and direction of the Steering Committee, lists every team role and action currently being fulfilled by a member of management prior to the empowerment of the team. Across from every item, responsibility is assigned to either an area manager, the elected team leader, the entire team through consensus decision making and/or some rotational system, or some other member of the organization (e.g., engineering, maintenance supervisor, employee resource coordinator). The date when that person is to take on that responsibility may also be identified if the responsibility is to be transferred at a later time (presumably after that person receives some orientation and training to accomplish the task). The responsibility may also be coded in a manner that lets team members know whether the person assigned has full decision-making responsibility (D) for it, has the responsibility to keep informed (I) about it, or has responsibility to support (S) actions taken by others regarding it. The column describing the responsibilities should include specific aspects relevant to the four functions of management—planning, organizing, leading, and controlling—as well as the ten roles described by Mintzberg. Other specific tasks formerly performed by the manager should also be listed. This may include items such as scheduling overtime, scheduling vacations, calling vendors and suppliers, performing maintenance, completing production reports, making job assignments, coordinating training, convening and chairing meetings, attending the meetings of other teams and/or management meetings, monitoring safety, preparing budget requests, coordinating housekeeping, preparing documentation, and allocating resources. In some organizations, the newly elected team leader and/or the team itself is also expected to review the performance of each team member and enforce the work rules, including the administration of disciplinary action when needed. However, more often than not, these functions are still kept within the domain of management. Exercise 10 provides a brief example of what such a Responsibility Chart might look like.

It is probably apparent that a team concept effort requires virtually everyone involved to think of themselves as a leader. Everyone

Table 9 Descriptions of Managerial Roles

Roles	Activities
Interpersonal	
Figurehead	Meeting the routine, obligatory social and legal duties required of the head of a unit. Examples would be attendance at social functions, meeting touring politicians, and lunching with buyers or suppliers.
Leader	Maintaining, developing, and motivating the human resources necessary to meet the needs of the unit.
Liaison	Developing and maintaining a network of individuals outside the unit in order to acquire information and actions of benefit to the unit.
Informational	
Monitor	Searching for and acquiring information about the unit and the environment the unit exists in so that the manager becomes an information center for the unit and the organization. This role derives from liaison and leader roles.
Disseminator	Distributing to others within the unit or organization selected information, some of which has been transformed through integration with other information.
Spokesperson	Distributing to others outside the unit or organization selected information regarding such things as the plans, values, and activities of the unit.
Decisional	
Entrepreneur	Proactive development and adjustment of the unit to take advantage of existing opportunities or meet anticipated changes in the environment. Actions are based on inferences and conclusions drawn from the evaluation and integration of information gathered in the monitor role.
Disturbance Handler	The reactive development of responses required to meet the immediate demands of the unit's environment. Examples of these demands would include a wildcat strike or the loss of major customer or supplier.
Resource Allocator	Evaluating and choosing among proposals, integrating activities, and authorizing activities and resource utilization.
Negotiator	Bargaining to acquire the resources to meet the needs of the unit and the organization.

EXERCISE 10

Clarifying Team Leadership Responsibility

Directions: Across from each responsibility listed below, mark the initials of the person who will be expected to fulfill that responsibility, the date when that expectation is to be activated, and whether the person responsible has decisional (D), informational (I), or support (S) level responsibility.

Responsibility	Leader	Members	Manager	Other
1. Scheduling				
2. Job assignments				
3. Training coordination				
4. Budget preparation				
5. Production reports				
6. Liaison with vendors				
7. Contact for "customers"				
8. Convener of meetings				
9. Safety				
10. Monitoring for quality				
11. Liaison with management				
12. Discipline				
13. Performance review				
14. Goal setting				
15. Product mix				
16. Motivating others				
16. Machine maintenance				
17. Housekeeping coordination				

EXERCISE 10 continued

Responsibility	Leader	Members	Manager	Other
18. Overtime requirements	_____	_____	_____	_____
19. Overhead allocations	_____	_____	_____	_____
20. Allocation of resources	_____	_____	_____	_____

has had some experience attempting to influence another person, a group, or some decision. Thus, by definition, we have all had some experience with leadership that we can learn from. Before a team conducts a role-clarification session to produce a Responsibility Chart and before it elects a leader, it would be helpful to hold a meeting or team training session to review what experience has taught each person about leadership. The session could begin with an open discussion of the best and worst leaders each team member has ever encountered. This discussion should be processed to identify what the team feels might represent the key do's and don'ts of effective leadership. Exercise 11 provides an activity that could be used to get each person on the team to think about themselves as leaders. This could be processed in a manner that emphasizes the wealth of leadership talent that exists on the team and the need for each member to fulfill some leadership functions. This could then be followed with the development of exercise 10 and possibly the election of a team leader. Note that the tone of this exercise session should be kept serious and positive. The exercise will help reveal the leadership talent that will help your organization succeed with its change efforts.

Summary

Members of effective teams know what is expected of them. They need to fulfill roles that include several tasks and assist in the process of working together as a unit. The ideal balance of differentiating roles sufficiently to let a member know what his or her priorities must be

EXERCISE 11

What Do You Know About Yourself as a Leader?

Directions: In this exercise, you will be asked to reflect on and share some perceptions of yourself as a leader. Research indicates that a key to leadership effectiveness is being particularly aware of your strengths as a leader. Thus, you will want to focus on what you see as your strengths—actual and potential—as a leader.

Each person in your group will be asked to take a turn in the "hot seat." When it is your turn, take five minutes to share with the group your perceptions of the questions listed below. First consider what a leader is by reading over the following definition: *A leader is anyone who influences a person or group to help change something.* Thus, a leader may or may not actually hold an official leadership position in an organization.

- What was a peak moment for you as a leader?
- What do you see as the strengths you bring (or could bring) to situations as a leader?
- What are the characteristics of your leadership style?
- What do you hope to be like as a leader a year from now?

The remaining group members should be excellent active listeners to the person sharing. Total undivided attention should be given to the person sharing. The person should be encouraged to share as much as possible about him or herself as a leader. The focus of attention should be kept on the leader who is sharing.

When the person has finished sharing his or her perceptions, the members should take five minutes to provide the leader with ample feedback, sharing their perceptions on:

- What did you hear the person share about his or her leadership strengths, style, experiences, and plans?
- What did you notice about the person as she or he shared personal information about leadership?
- What did you learn about leadership from listening to the person today and/or any contact you may have had with him or her in the past?

while allowing for the flexibility to meet situational needs is difficult to maintain. This chapter provided two approaches for achieving clarity and balance. The role of leader must also be fulfilled. Sometimes this means one person—a manager, team leader, or coach—is to fulfill the role. In order to take teams seriously, the person fulfilling the leadership role must use a style that is conducive to teams. The style must involve people and build commitment to the work that needs to be done. Sometimes the role of leader is diffused and all the members are expected to take on parts of the role. Thus, the leadership function is fulfilled as a team. This generally requires knowledge of and consistent follow-through on procedures agreed to by all team members. Next we'll turn our attention to establishing effective and efficient team procedures.

Reasonable and Efficient Operating Procedures

P assing plays in football require that every player (e.g., the guards, backs, wide receivers) uses his or her talents differently than if a running play were called. The goal is basically the same, but the players are counting on their teammates to execute actions in a precise manner. Confidence in the team and trust between teammates grows when everyone can rely on each other. Work teams also need some structured and disciplined approaches to their tasks. The task assigned to a team may require a certain set of procedures. Teams need procedures to plan, schedule, budget, set goals, hold meetings, share information, make decisions, identify and resolve problems, and evaluate progress. These procedures must be effective enough to live up to established standards. They must also be efficient enough to avoid the problems of fatigue and boredom. The purpose of this chapter is to examine some of the key procedures most teams need to utilize and recommend processes that will help develop these procedures.

Using Systematic Problem-Solving Procedures

Perhaps the most important procedure a team needs to commit to using is a systematic approach to problem solving. Once established, the team can use its problem-solving procedures to solve the problems in all of its other procedures. There are many good models that outline the steps of problem solving. I have seen teams use "The 10-step road map to problem solving"; "The 8Ds of problem solving"; I've even seen a team use a manual that provided a fifty-two-point check-list to ensure a systematic approach to problem solving. Unfortunately, team members typically have trouble remembering the 8Ds, let alone a fifty-two-step model. Team members typically respond positively to training sessions dedicated to problem solving but fail to systematical-ly apply the model on a regular basis on the job.

The 4-A Problem-Solving Model

After reviewing the literature, I have come to the conclusion that there are basically four key steps to problem solving. I have labeled each step with a word that begins with the letter "A" to make them easier to remember. Within each step, the team first expands its thinking. At the end of the step, it focuses or narrows its thinking. Table 10 outlines what I call the 4-A problem-solving model. I have trained hundreds of teams using this model and have found that team members remember the steps and succeed at systematic problem solving.

Awareness

The first "A" of the 4-A problem-solving model stands for *awareness*. The team must broaden its thinking by listing all the possible prob-lems it might have to deal with. It is often useful to apply the rules of brainstorming to ensure that you have identified the whole range of problems that might deserve attention. Do not criticize the consid-eration of any problem or engage in a discussion of any problem at this point. Concentrate instead on developing as complete a list as possible. The following list will help a team make the most of a brainstorming session:

- Clarify the question or issue that the group is going to use the brainstorming technique on and the rules the group will use to get the most out of brainstorming.
- Take some time as a group to think before speaking. Each indi-vidual should write notes regarding the ideas she or he has on the matter. No individual should self-censor any idea that is relevant to the issue.
- Allow anyone to just blurt out ideas as they feel like it, or the group can sit in a circle and go around the group, with each person being allowed to contribute ideas as long as they haven't already been

Table 10 The 4-A Problem-Solving Model

Awareness

Expand your thinking to consider all the possible problems by
　　Using brainstorming
　　Charting all ideas
　　Not criticizing or discussing things during this time

Narrow your focus to the one problem you will work on now by
　　Using criteria to review each problem
　　Writing a one-sentence problem statement

Analysis

Expand your thinking to all the possible causes by
　　Gathering data
　　Using brainstorming or fishbone diagramming

Narrow your focus to the one to three core causes of the problem by
　　Using criteria to review each possible cause
　　Applying the Pareto Principle to pick the significant few causes
　　Highlighting the chief cause(s)

Alternatives

Expand thinking to all the solutions to the chief causes by
　　Providing individual quiet time to write down ideas
　　Encouraging creative thinking
　　Using round-robin brainstorming
　　Pooling ideas and "hitchhiking" on each others' ideas

Narrow the focus to the best strategy available by
　　Using criteria (e.g., effectiveness, cost) to screen solutions
　　Seeking consensus decision making rather than majority rule
　　Ensuring the strategy addresses the chief causes

Actions

Expand thinking to all the possible implementation actions by
　　Specifying what might need to happen in concrete terms
　　Ensuring the strategy is real, not just philosophical

Narrow the focus to who is to do what with whom and by when by
　　Clarifying individual responsibilities
　　Charting an implementation time line
　　Stating indicators that will verify the problem is solved

---

introduced. However, people should be encouraged to build on previously reported ideas by offering variations and more specifics.

■ Have someone write each idea down, ideally on a flip chart, so that everyone can see the list as it grows. This will show respect to each person, help reduce redundancy, and provide a visual stimulus that may trigger additional ideas.

- Make sure there is a firm rule that absolutely no criticism of any idea is allowed to be given during the brainstorming period. The group is seeking quantity now and will deal with the quality of ideas later. No one should verbally criticize, evaluate, judge, or debate any idea offered. Likewise, no one should groan, roll their eyes, snicker, or make any other sounds or nonverbal gestures that might infer criticism of any idea offered.
- Create an atmosphere of positive enthusiasm that surrounds the effort. Even when you are brainstorming a list of problems, it helps if the group recognizes how well it understands the situation, as evidenced by the long list of issues/problems it was capable of generating. The fact that the group has much collective wisdom should be reinforced.

After a long, long list of problems has been identified, the team needs to review the list to decide which problem (or problems) deserve priority attention. Some criteria should be used when screening the list. For example, you might give priority attention to all problems that are both important *and* something the team actually can influence on its own. Then, pick the problem you will focus on first and write a one- or two-sentence definition of the problem. The section below on problem selection provides some suggestions on how to select a problem to work on. The next section on prioritizing procedures provides suggestions for how a group can begin the process of narrowing the list of problems. Ultimately, the team should attempt to achieve a consensus decision regarding its priority problems. A consensus decision means that every team member agrees with the logic underlying the decision and promises to fully support the actions related to the decision. Suggestions on how to achieve consensus decisions will be provided later in this chapter.

Problem Selection

After generating a long, long list of the many possible problems the group is aware of, the group should narrow its focus. Ideally, the group will be allowed to work on one problem at a time and achieve a high-quality, systematic approach to problem analysis and resolution. At the very least, the group needs to sort through the problems it generated during the first part of the Awareness step, outlined in table 10, eliminating the redundant items and then listing the problems in some sort of priority order. This can best be accomplished by systematically screening the list of problems using some previously agreed-upon criteria and then using some voting procedure to determine the rank order of issues. Some criteria that could be used to help a group think through the merits of each potential problem include:

■ Is the problem within the guidelines of what teams at this location are allowed to work on?

■ Do the people on this team have the specialized knowledge needed to understand this problem? Does anyone on this team have the authority to address this problem?

■ Is the team likely to learn a lot by tackling this problem—about the subject matter of the problem, how to work together on a team, and the 4-A problem solving method?

■ How bothersome (or costly) is this problem now? To whom?

■ How important is this problem to this team? To management? To the union? To others?

■ To what extent does this problem affect the performance of people's jobs? The quality of the product or service? Profitability? Timeliness of production? Customer satisfaction?

■ To what extent does this problem affect the satisfaction of people working here?

■ Is this a problem that can be solved quickly?

■ Is this a problem that is significant and yet something the members of this team can do something about?

Prioritizing Procedures

After the team has reviewed each of the problems that appeared on the original brainstormed list using one or more of the criteria suggested above, the team must pick which problem it will work on first.

There are many methods that a team can use to prioritize problems. Ultimately, you may want your team to reach a consensus decision on such issues, but the team may benefit from using one of the procedures listed below to get a feel for the general thinking of the team:

■ Rank order all items.

■ Give everyone five votes (or some other set number) and then rank order the problems according to the number of votes received.

- Discuss each problem one at a time. Then have each person rate the problem on a one to ten scale for each criteria to be used to make the decision. Add up the scores for each problem and use the scores to rank order the problems.
- Categorize the problems into three lists: (1) hot items that must be addressed by this team immediately, (2) important items that the group needs to start researching very soon but will take some time to address, and (3) wish list items that seem important but may not be addressed. Then eliminate all other items and vote to select the top priorities in categories 1 and 2.
- Identify five (or some other set number) problems that your group is capable of and motivated to address. Then submit your list to the authority figures to whom you will be reporting and ask them to prioritize the list.
- Eliminate all the items that are not appropriate for your group to address. Write a problem statement for each item your group is capable of addressing and is motivated to address. Place each of the statements in a jar (or box or hat) and randomly draw the problem statement that the group will work on first.

Whatever method you use, the group should end up being focused on which problem it will address. Every person on the team must commit to addressing the problem, even if it wasn't his or her first choice. Finally, the problem must be stated clearly so that all group meetings are used to analyze and resolve this problem, not all the other problems, even though those other problems may also be very important.

Exercise 12 provides an example of how a team went through this first step of the 4-A model to address problems it was having with the procedures it used to operate as a team. They brainstormed a list of the procedures they felt they might need to have to be a highly effective team. They then chose three criteria to review their list: *effectiveness, efficiency* and *importance.* They rated each of the potential procedure problems using each of the criteria (0 = not at all; 1 = a little bit; 2 = somewhat; 3 = to a large extent; 4 = very much). They created a "problem-priority score" by adding the first two scores together (effectiveness and efficiency) and then multiplying that number by the weight assigned to the third score (importance). The procedural problems with the three lowest problem priority scores were then addressed using the remaining steps of the 4-A model.

EXERCISE 12

Becoming Aware of Your Team's Procedural Problems

Directions: Rate the procedures under each question with the appropriate number as follows: 0 = not at all; 1 = a little bit; 2 = somewhat; 3 = to a large extent; 4 = very much. Create your own "problem-priority score" by adding the first two columns together (effectively and efficiently) and then multiplying the total by the score in the third column. You might consider systematically applying the 4-A problem-solving model to the three procedures that receive the lowest scores.

Procedures Used By Your Team	How effectively does your team perform this procedure?	How efficiently does your team perform this procedure?	How important is this procedure to your team?
Planning			
Scheduling			
Budgeting			
Goal setting			
Meetings			
Information sharing			
Decision making			
Problem identification			
Problem analysis			
Solution generation			
Solution selection			
Implementation			
Task assignment			
Progress evaluation			
Other			

Analysis

The second "A" of the 4-A problem-solving model stands for *analysis*. The team now needs to broaden its thinking by brainstorming all the potential causes of the problem that it has defined. It may be helpful to use a technique such as the *fishbone diagramming* method to ensure that the group has covered all the likely categories of the problem's causes. The fishbone method suggests that you draw the skeleton of a fish and imagine that the backbone represents the problem.

After you have a long list of all the possible causes of the problem, systematically analyze each cause to clarify the extent to which it actually contributes to the problem you are focusing on. This may necessitate gathering some data and charting it in a systematic manner. The Pareto Principle states that although all problems have multiple causes, a few significant causes are probably at the root of the problem. You are thus attempting to sort out the significant few causes from the trivial many. The team is to eventually identify the one (or two or three) root causes that if addressed would generate a very significant reduction of the problem. Remember, you are trying to identify causes, not solutions at this stage. Following are some suggestions on how to conduct this second step of the 4-A problem solving model.

Problem Analysis Techniques

As in all the steps, the group must first expand its thinking to determine the many perspectives that might help explain why the problem exists. Brainstorming might again be useful. However, two other techniques tend to also be helpful. One of these is data collecting, or charting. In this technique, people simply note each time the problem occurs and what preceded its occurrence. If you use charting, you must do this systematically. Team members must be perceptive, vigilant, and thorough. It must be determined what data will be tracked and how it will be measured. Some sampling procedures may need to be learned if the kind of problem being addressed occurs frequently.

Another method now used by many problem-solving teams is called fishbone diagramming, briefly mentioned earlier, in which a drawing of a fish skeleton is made. In this technique, you should think of the backbone of a fish as the problem and each of the main bones that branch off of the backbone as categories of the problem's causes. A common system of generating these "bones" is known as the

4-M (or 5-M plus e) method. The M's refer to manpower, materials, machines, and methods (plus measurements and environment in the 5-M plus e version). The group asks, "What about the people (manpower) surrounding the occurrence of the problem? What are they doing, or not doing, that might be causing the problem?" The group asks other questions relevant to each of these Ms. Each answer is charted on the fishbone diagram, thus organizing a review of the many possible causes to the problem. Additional "bones" are added to the diagram for causes that are not easily categorized via the 4-M's.

Although all problems have multiple causes, some causes are significant and others are trivial. The Pareto Principle suggests that 80 percent of any problem is caused by 20 percent of its causes. The group must now focus on the root causes. It must determine which elements are most likely to cause the problem and/or have the greatest impact on the problem. There are other statistically based approaches for determining which causes are most significant. You could also use the voting procedures discussed below. Whatever method you use, remember that your group must identify the chief cause (or two or three). The idea is to achieve continuous improvement. Most problems cannot be totally eliminated. The task is to identify the cause that, if eliminated, would make such a significant improvement that it would make this problem-solving effort worthwhile.

Alternatives

The third "A" of the 4-A problem-solving method stands for *alternatives*. The team needs to free up its creative potential, suspend all judgment, and identify a long list of the many strategies and approaches that it might take to address the root cause (or causes) of the problem it is attempting to solve. There should not be any discussion or debate of the alternatives you dream up until you have all the possibilities charted on your list. There are many blockages that may interfere with a team's effort to creatively identify possible solutions to problems. Some common obstacles to creativity include:

- Fear of looking foolish
- Fear of risk taking
- Fear of retaliation
- Looking for the "right" (perfect) answers
- Not believing you are creative
- Taking a wait-and-see attitude

- Fear of getting blamed
- Fear of getting stuck with doing the work
- Having a culture that doesn't allow for a playful spirit
- Overemphasis on being practical
- Overemphasis on being logical
- Cynicism
- Inability to tolerate ambiguity
- Lack of trust
- Working with a group that agrees on things too quickly

Assuming that the group has been able to overcome these inhibitors to creativity, it must now use some criteria to identify the one (or two or three) key strategies it would attempt to utilize to eliminate the causes underlying the problem it chose to resolve. Narrowing the alternatives can be accomplished by using the same voting procedures described previously in the Prioritizing Procedures section. Ultimately, it is important that the team reach a consensus decision to select the strategy it will use to solve the problem.

Action

The fourth "A" of the 4-A problem solving method stands for *action*. Too many problem solvers stop after they have identified the solution to a problem and fail to detail a plan for how to implement that solution. A team should identify the many actions that may need to be taken to operationalize the strategy selected as the best way to eliminate the problem. After all the actions and steps have been identified, it should be specified who is to do what with whom, by when, and how in order to achieve a solution. Obviously, the team must follow up on this plan in order to solve the problem. Exercise 13 provides a form that teams can use to document their systematic use of the 4-A problem-solving model.

Making Effective and Efficient Decisions

Throughout the previous section on problem solving, it was suggested that the team should ideally make a consensus decision at the end of each step of the 4-A problem-solving model. It is not easy to reach consensus decisions. Do not insist that every decision be a consensus decision. This would wear out most groups. Sometimes an authority figure (by nature of position, expertise, or passion regarding the

EXERCISE 13

The Problem-Solving Team Report

Directions: Respond to the questions to document your team's use of the 4-A problem-solving model.

1. How many problems was your team able to think of during the brainstorming of the awareness step? Provide a copy of the list of potential problems your team came up with.

2. What criteria were used to choose the problem the team will work on?

   Provide a one-sentence definition of the problem you selected.

   _____

3. How many causes of the problem was your team able to think of during the first half of the analysis step?

   Provide a copy of the list or the fishbone diagram of potential causes of the problem your team selected to work on.

4. Using the same criteria listed in question 2 above, what did your team choose as the one (or two or three) chief cause of the problem?

5. How many solutions was your team able to think of during the brainstorming of the alternatives step? Provide a copy of the list of potential solutions to the chief causes of the problem your team has chosen to resolve.

6. Using the same criteria listed in question 2 above, what did your team choose as the most effective, efficient, and afford-able alternative (solution) available?

7. Provide a copy of the details of an action plan that would need to be followed in order to implement your team's solution to the problem. Be sure your plan makes it very clear *what* would take place, *who* would need to be involved, *how* members of your team would be involved in the implementation process, and *when* each step would be completed.

decision) should be allowed to make the decision after hearing all points of view. Sometimes you should resort to a voting system in which either a majority decides or perhaps a two-thirds or three-fourths majority is reached before the decision is finalized. Use these approaches on less important issues. The group should not use these methods as a way of avoiding working together as a full team. Although time pressures may require resorting to a method that takes less time to reach a decision, avoid allowing poor planning to create these time pressures.

The benefits of getting everyone to buy into a decision are great. Consensus decisions promote commitment and a full sense of team. They typically take longer to reach but save the team the time of having to explain the decision (its rationale and its implementation plan) after the fact. Research studies clearly indicate that a consensus decision is better than what the average individual would make. It may even be better than the decision anyone in the group could make if the members truly build on each others' ideas rather than set up a competition and work toward a compromise that will satisfy the majority. The whole will be greater than the sum of the parts when team members are open to the variety of perspectives available on the team, emphasizing the useful parts of several ideas, and creating solutions to problems that no individual alone could have created. A group has reached a consensus decision when every person in the group buys into the logic underlying the decision and is willing to defend it as if it were his or her own. Some suggestions for how teams can reach consensus decisions include:

- Clearly identify periods of time when the group is going to brainstorm and strictly enforce the rule of no criticism during the brainstorming session.
- Look for common ground to begin the discussion of options and build upon this.
- Argue/discuss the logic underlying each element but avoid arguing for your own point of view simply to "win" the point. The purpose is for the *team* to win, not an individual.
- Celebrate differences! It is important that some group member periodically remind the group of the benefits of having differing points of view, even during heated points in the discussion.
- Do not use averaging (e.g., "You say we need ten units and I say we can only get six units. Let's split the difference and ask for eight"), trading of influence (e.g., "I'll support you on this one if you'll support me on the next one"), or random methods (e.g., drawing a solution out of a hat) to break deadlocks.
- If you use voting procedures at all, make it clear that you are just taking a straw poll with no binding effect just to see how close the

group is to consensus. If only one or two people do not fully support the trial balloon, ask them what could be added to the solution to get them to fully support the decision. However, be aware that any voting procedure could generate some political dynamics within the team, resulting in either some less-than-rational solutions or some people merely complying with their teammates requests rather than giving a true commitment.

- Beware of time pressures. Manage the time at meetings so that the team dedicates more time to the most important issues.

- Use procedures to ensure that each person has time to speak, everyone listens, and everyone provides clear feedback verifying the degree to which they understand the discussion.

- Sometimes, when you get stuck on an issue, you may need to table it and come back to it at a later time.

- Be suspicious of early, quick, easy agreements. Is the group avoiding conflict? Are team members truly committed to implementing the decision? Be sure that every team member clearly demonstrates agreement (e.g., verbally agrees or nods his or her head in agreement). Do not allow silence to infer agreement!

Using Meetings Effectively and Efficiently

The greatest fear I have when I am a member of a team is how much time will be wasted in meetings. I do not deny that face-to-face communications are crucial for team success and, thus, that meetings are a necessity. I have just experienced too many "get togethers" that were left so unstructured that those people who needed some attention talked, very few people listened, and there appeared to be no focus to the meeting. Considering the billions of hours spent in meetings every year in this country and the average salary of the people spending their time in them, meetings are probably the most expensive social technology utilized in businesses today. A return needs to be made on this investment if we are going to build effective teams.

Meetings should have a purpose or they shouldn't be held. Some meetings may have more than one purpose. Sometimes each item on the agenda of a meeting has a different purpose. One of the main keys to making meetings effective is to clarify the purpose to each attendee before the meeting is held. Basically, the five reasons to have a meeting are to:

1. Share information
2. Discuss issues
3. Reach decisions on issues
4. Build relations
5. Fulfill a commitment

The behavior of the team members should match the purpose of the meeting. For example, if the purpose is to merely share information, members should take notes and ask questions of clarification. If the purpose of the meeting is to decide issues, the members should come to the meeting prepared and systematically apply a problem-solving model (e.g., the 4-A problem-solving model described in the previous section) to guide the discussion. Members should also know what role each of them is expected to play at the meeting. There are three sets of roles to consider: job title (task) related roles, group dynamics roles, and meeting management roles. We discussed strategies to help a team clarify the task and group dynamics roles in the previous chapter. The meeting management roles are described next.

Meeting Management Roles

The Chairperson (Leader)

The chairperson convenes the meeting, announces the agenda, and works to keep the group's discussion in line with the meeting's agenda. She or he is expected to contribute to the discussion of the agenda items in addition to helping ensure that an orderly discussion takes place. This person frequently acts as the contact person for team members between meetings and may serve as the spokesperson for the team to relay the information generated at the meeting to other groups and individuals.

The Recorder

The recorder produces written documentation of the team's work at the meeting. She or he takes the minutes and is expected to at least accurately record all decisions made by the team. It should be clarified in advance whether the recorder is also expected to document the points made during the discussions at the meeting or whether the discussion should remain off the record in order to encourage an honest and open exchange of views. It is often useful for the recorder to attempt to capture this information on large newsprint sheets of paper so that all team members can see what is being documented. This demonstrates that the ideas are being heard, provides an ongoing opportunity to ensure that points are being perceived accurately, and tends to reduce the likelihood that other team members will repeat the same points already expressed by others.

The Facilitator

The facilitator may be a team member taking on this role for a given meeting or may be an outsider asked to sit in with the team and help the process of the meeting. The facilitator is not to comment on any of the content of the ideas generated and is not to generate content ideas him or herself without announcing that she or he is temporarily stepping out of the facilitator role. The facilitator observes the group's dynamics to determine if participation levels are being appropriately managed, that the group's ground rules and procedures are being systematically applied, and that team members are fulfilling the roles they pledged to meet. The things a facilitator should look for in a group and how she or he should feed back group process observations was addressed in previous chapters. To contribute to group discussions, facilitators can:

- Clearly state the purpose of the discussion
- Clarify the time available and recruit someone to help monitor the time during the discussion
- Recruit someone to chart the comments generated by the group or at least to take notes
- Encourage the group to agree on a procedure or strategy on how to discuss the topic before the discussion begins (e.g., "Should we brainstorm all our ideas before we critique them?"; "Should we go around the circle allowing each member to speak?")
- Encourage people not to just sit back and listen but to provide input without dominating
- Not comment on every person's comments
- Beware of "handclasp" decisions
- Directly invite input from "silent" members

- Summarize/clarify perceptions of what the group has discussed and/or agreed to every fifteen minutes or so
- Share with the group what they personally got out of the discussion —what they heard, noticed, and learned

Members

Every group member has the responsibility to come to meetings prepared, abide by any ground rules or norms established by the team, contribute to team discussions, not disturb other members with side conversations, and follow through on assignments. Teams should, at some point, hold a meeting about meetings and decide what they need to do to operate effectively. Then if members behave in a manner consistent with the conclusions reached about the responsibilities of team members at meetings, trust levels will grow and meetings should become more effective and efficient.

The Representative

Some members may be assigned or elected to another team in order for their constituency group to be heard and/or kept informed. It is the responsibility of a representative to solicit input in advance of the meeting and serve his or her constituents at the meeting. However, the team may have goals that are superordinate to the several stakeholder groups represented at the meeting. In this case, this type of member needs to participate in decision making for the good of the overall organization while still attending to the needs of his or her constituency. It is easy to say in a book, "Do the right thing!" However, the political realities of organizational life complicate decisions. The stronger the commitment to the team's goals, the fewer problems should occur. It is naive and not recommended to believe that there should be no "politics" in team meetings. Perhaps the best ethical guide is what Cavanaugh, Moberg, and Velasquez (1981) recommend: Try to ensure that the political behaviors do not take away the basic rights of people as members of our society. It is true that the more people see a team making decisions that are more politically based than rational, the less faith they will have in the team concept. If we are going to take teams seriously, we must strive to balance the realities of conflicting interests and the goals of the teams. We must be realistic enough to recognize the human nature of political behavior and the value of logical decision making.

The Resource Person

At some point, the team may recognize that a certain base of knowledge or skill is needed to analyze or solve a particular problem. The team may not need a permanent member with that particular knowledge/skill base. It should invite someone with the expertise to attend one or more meetings and provide the team with what is needed. Typically, this person is to have "voice, not a vote." That is, she or he does not have a say in the final decision but is there to provide information. It is important that team members treat this resource person with respect. I have seen teams invite someone to be their resource person (e.g., an engineer) only to blame the person for why a certain problem exists. Resource people should be treated as invited guests. Gain information in as descriptive a manner as possible. Reserve discussion of criticism of that person's functional area for a closed-door session without that person present. More will be said about the need for teams to develop constructive external relationships in chapter 10.

The Observer

Organizations may launch teams as pilot projects. The plan may call for the launch of other teams at a later date. It may be useful to have people from other parts of a facility sit in on a team meeting to get a feel for how teams work. Even if teams have already been spread throughout the organization, it may help to exchange ideas of methods to improve the use of teams by having members of other teams sit in on various meetings. Typically, there should be a rule that this visitor should have neither a voice nor vote. They should merely be there to observe and learn. At the end of the meeting, they could be given some time to ask questions of the whole group or of a certain team member. In general, guard against allowing these observers to act as evaluators of teams. Also guard against recommending someone to sit in on a certain team because "they do it right." The value that may be promoted through these observations is that we all can learn from each other. Don't expect each group to hold its meetings just like every other group. Assume each group should have some unique characteristics but that we can expand our thinking about how to improve group meetings by visiting other groups. Again, this is part of a strategy to promote constructive external relations between groups, which will be discussed in detail in chapter 10.

Analyzing Your Meetings

Perhaps you have already recognized that the advice provided in this section on improving teams follows the basic model of teams, that is, identify the goals/purpose, clarify the roles, and verify whether the talent needed to complete the task exists. In order to further this, you may want to now use the 4-A problem-solving model to solve the problems occurring at your team's meetings. Exercise 14 provides a useful starting point for becoming aware of a large range of the problems your team may be having with its meetings. It is a simple survey to be filled out by all team members; the results can be summarized and fed back at a session dedicated to analyzing the team's meetings.

Improving Informal Procedures

So far we have looked at the team's procedures for problem solving, decision making, and holding meetings. Teams may have to work on several other important procedures (e.g., scheduling, budgeting) in order to be effective and efficient. It is not the purpose of this chapter to provide tools to improve every conceivable procedure, but it is hoped that a team will apply a systematic problem-solving procedure such as the 4-A problem-solving model to resolve its other formal procedural problems. However, every team also develops procedures for doing things that are not written down anywhere and are often never even talked about. These assumed ways of doing things are usually referred to as group norms. Every team has its own norms. These are rules and standards that are unwritten and usually unspoken. Once you have been on a team for a while, you learn what it is okay to do and what it is not, who to go to for what, how hard you should work and how seriously you should take your work, what is approriate to wear to work and what is not, and who you can break with and who you can't. Some examples of team norms are:

- "It's more important to get it done than to do it right."
- "Stay out of other people's belongings."
- "It's not cool to volunteer."
- "When the boss is away, so-and-so is in charge."
- "It's not okay to blow your own horn."
- "It's not okay to snitch on a teammate."

EXERCISE 14

Team Meeting Questionnaire

Directions: Use the following checklist to rate the strengths and weaknesses of the meetings you attend and participate in. For all items, circle the rating that is most accurate for the situation described, with 1 = it fails on the dimension, 2 = it sometimes fulfills the dimension, and 3 = it succeeds on this dimension in most ways.

Is the purpose of the meeting clarified in advance?	1	2	3
Is an agenda provided in advance?	1	2	3
Is the agenda followed during the meeting?	1	2	3
Is it clear who is or is not expected to attend?	1	2	3
Do the members attend regularly? Are they tardy?	1	2	3
Is the physical space set up to fulfill the meeting's purpose?	1	2	3
Are meetings interrupted?	1	2	3
Do the members come to the meetings prepared?	1	2	3
Do enough members participate actively enough?	1	2	3
Do members understand their roles and responsibilities?	1	2	3
Is the time scheduled for the meeting conducive to its purpose?	1	2	3
Do members listen to each other?	1	2	3
Does the leader or chair fulfill his or her role?	1	2	3
Do members reflect on the process of the meeting?	1	2	3
Do members seem to be acting on hidden agendas?	1	2	3
Does the group overdepend on the leader or facilitator?	1	2	3
Is the amount of material covered at each meeting appropriate?	1	2	3
Are minutes of the meeting put into writing?	1	2	3
Do the minutes accurately summarize the meetings?	1	2	3
Are the meeting minutes distributed appropriately?	1	2	3
Is there follow-through after meetings?	1	2	3
Are ground rules and norms clear and adhered to?	1	2	3
Is the effectiveness of the meetings evaluated?	1	2	3

EXERCISE 15

The Unwritten Rules of Your Team

Directions: Each individual team member should reveal what she or he thinks are the unwritten rules of the team. Each norm that is reported should be written down. Once the list is completed, the whole team needs to decide what it wants to do with each norm that has been identified. Then the norms should be rated by putting an "A" in front of the norms your team wants to keep and live up to; a "B" in front of the norms your team wants to modify, and then rewrite it to reflect what you want it to be; and a "C" in front of the norms your team wants to drop or doesn't believe in. Once the norms are all rated, the team can then add to the list any new norms it wants to try to live up to over the next year.

These become expected patterns of behavior, some of which may serve the team well, while others should be examined and revised. Exercise 15 outlines an approach to examining these informal procedures.

Summary

Teams need reasonable and efficient procedures in order to fulfill their goals, utilize their talent, and fulfill their roles. Perhaps the most important procedure is a team's approach to problem solving. A systematic approach to problem solving can help a team complete its tasks and can be applied to efforts to improve all of its other procedures. A disciplined approach to utilizing procedures not only addresses task concerns but also provides a great opportunity to build and maintain trust and confidence. Confidence comes from successfully applying our plans and our talents. Trust is a matter of doing what we said we were going to do. In the next chapter, we will examine how trust affects another key component of effective teams, namely, constructive interpersonal relationships.

CHAPTER 8

Constructive Interpersonal Relationships

E ven if every team member clearly knows and understands the goals of the team and is talented and knows each team member's roles and responsibilities and there is a great set of procedures for working together, the team could become ineffective and dissatisfying if team members do not get along well enough with each other. All it takes is for a couple of key members to get into an ego conflict and the dynamics can turn team efforts sour. Team building requires a balance of task-oriented and relationship-oriented developmental opportunities. Perhaps too many team-building programs have gone overboard on the relationship-building aspects. Team building has a reputation for being a "touchy–feely" experience that many managers and their direct reports alike dread. Nevertheless, it should be made clear that something must be done to gain a positive, accepting, constructive approach to each team member as a person. Adversarial or apathetic relations can destroy a team. The elements of "good" relationships, effective communications, dynamics of personalities, and constructive conflict resolution will be discussed in this chapter.

Developing Good Relationships

There is no universal standard for good relationships, and there are no objective tests to verify if members are treating each other well enough. It is possible, however, to identify some key elements that identify or are a sign of good relationships. These elements include:

- Trust
- Mutual respect; lack of prejudice; accepting differences
- Open and honest communications, especially effective listening
- Efforts to resolve conflicts constructively
- An understanding and acceptance of each other's roles and goals
- Keeping "politics" to a minimum; having no hidden agendas
- Not allowing badmouthing/backstabbing of others
- Adequate interaction with each other
- A willingness to try new things
- Following through on promises
- Seeking input and involvement in decision making
- Having relatively equal power
- Reliability/dependability
- A focus on issues and interests, not personalities or positions
- Recognition of mutual interests
- A willingness to generate options
- A sense of fairness
- Actions to promote a long-term relationship
- Balance of emotionality and rationality
- Efforts to build commitment rather than gain compliance

Building and Maintaining Trust

The "secret" to developing and maintaining trust is simple but not easy. Trust is basically a function of reliability. You can trust an enemy if the person is reliable and predictable. You don't have to like someone to trust them. Trust comes from seeing people do what they said they were going to do. Trust is developed through actions, not words. Words can convince you to believe/have faith that the person might be trustworthy, but actions are needed to verify whether that faith was well placed. The statement, "Just trust me on this one," has been violated so many times that it has become a standard joke.

If you want team members to trust you, simply say you are going to do something and then do it. If this cycle is repeated often enough, people will trust you. While this is simple, it won't be easy for several reasons. People are not machines. Thus, we are not as consistent in our actions as we would logically assume we should be. Some people have long memories and may focus on the few times that you failed to follow through on your promises. You may have to make it clear to these people that you are trying to become more reliable. Make very small promises, but make very visible efforts to follow through on those promises. Encourage all team members to do the same. The team concept should not be sold in such a manner that infers that it will be the solution to all of the team's problems. Make small promises about team activities and benefits and then follow through on those promises. Trust is a sacred commodity and it must be renewed by people seeing the consistency between actions and words.

Providing Respect

Aretha Franklin spelled it out to us over the years, and we all need it. All we have to do is provide a little respect. Trust takes some time to build; respect is something we can provide immediately. If you genuinely want to show more respect to others, it is just a matter of will. Respect is showing honor and consideration to others. It is based on the assumption that others are valuable. Again, you do not have to like someone in order to demonstrate respect to the person, though it would make it a lot easier. Showing respect indicates that you do not believe you should be judging the worth of others as people. You may or may not think they are the best accountants or managers, for example, but you believe that they are to be honored as people.

You must show respect in order for it to have a positive impact on relationships. The basic way we show respect to others is by listening to them. However, it appears that most adults in the world of work are terrible listeners. We feel so busy that we don't have the patience to listen. We want to get our point across, so we sell our ideas rather than attend to what the other person is saying. Young children start out as naturally good listeners. They repeat back what their parents say, sometimes to the chagrin of the adults. But somewhere along the way in the growing-up process, we begin to jump to responses like "right," "wrong," "agree," "disagree." Somewhere we hear the message, "You're not listening to me!" and know it really means, "You're not obeying me!" We fail to describe what we hear and instead emphasize evaluation, interpretation, and agreement or disagreement. We need to reclaim the understanding that listening is a two-phase process: description, then judgment; data gathering, then decision making. Listening to someone does not mean you necessarily agree with what they are saying, it is simply a matter of showing respect for them. Exercise 16 provides some tips for improving listening skills.

EXERCISE 16

Tips on Being a Good Listener

Directions: Read through the list below and circle the items you are willing to commit to improving in your efforts to provide respect to the members of teams you are working with.

1. First, you must really want to listen!

2. Pay attention and show you are paying attention.

3. Listen for content and then for meaning. Describe what you hear and then attempt to state what that means to you and how you react to it.

4. Try not to interrupt too often.

5. Try not to argue mentally.

6. Feelings are not "right" or "wrong," so avoid telling the person, "You should or shouldn't feel (upset, happy, sad)."

7. Remember who you are responding to and take their needs into account.

8. When you do make a judgment statement, separate what you think of the person from what you think of the person's behavior or opinions.

9. Be aware of "nonverbal" signals.

10. Clarify things and check things out instead of making assumptions.

11. It is sometimes helpful to report your own feelings. This can create a supportive and open atmosphere. However, beware of tendencies to steal the spotlight.

12. Remember, you will never be a perfect listener. However, this does not mean you shouldn't make a significant effort to improve your listening abilities.

Improving Communications

Trust and respect are key attitudes that people demonstrate and thus influence interpersonal relationships. Communication skills are the key relationship-building behaviors that people need to develop and utilize with their teammates. Basically, communication is a matter of sharing information, listening effectively, and providing constructive feedback. These skills are so basic and fundamental that they must be emphasized and reinforced through every team-building effort.

Successful baseball, basketball, and football coaches have been known to stress the fundamentals. Your team or committee needs to stress the fundamentals of communication. What "drills" or "warm-up exercises" can help the team practice the fundamentals? My favorite is designed to get each member to reflect on what experience has taught them about topics relevant to their team-building efforts. It gets each member to use a process whereby the person in the "hot seat" *shares information* about such things as their experiences with teams, work, leadership, and conflict and then asks them to reflect on what they learned from each of these experiences. The content of what is to be shared should be varied to reflect on the issues the team is attempting to address. Asking each person to reflect on the lessons learned from experiences reminds people that experience is the best teacher, but only when they are aware of what is to be learned from the experience. The remaining team members are to demonstrate their best *listening skills* while the person shares. After the person sharing has revealed his or her experiences and the lessons learned for up to five minutes, the team members should bombard the person with *feedback*. The members should structure their feedback in such a way that they first describe literally what they heard and noticed, then interpret what it meant to them, and, finally, what they learned or relearned through the exercise. Members are encouraged to act as a feedback team and not wait to take turns before feeding back what the person shared. Thus, the process provides a practice of the three key skills, and the content provides potentially valuable wisdom to be applied to issues facing the team. Exercise 17, "The Icebreaker," provides a sample version of this activity.

I find that the key to getting people to improve their abilities to share information is mainly a function of practice. It may feel awkward and painful to be in the hot seat for five minutes, but it is rewarding to have your experiences listened to and valued. To have constructive interpersonal relationships on a team, members must be willing to self-disclose. Self-esteem and self-confidence issues might interfere with the delivery of information. Provision of self-improvement options such as a Dale Carnegie course might help certain individuals and supplement the team-building effort. The "coach" may also have to spend some energy ensuring that the climate is safe for such sharing during team sessions. The respect provided by effective listening should help. Perhaps the group can focus on the listening

EXERCISE 17

The Icebreaker

Directions: Each member of the team is to take on the role of information sharer while the other members listen intently. After five minutes of sharing, team members are to give feedback to the person utilizing the guidelines listed below:

The role of the person sharing

- Share your experiences in as constructive a manner as possible. After each experience that you share, state what you learned from that experience that perhaps shapes your approach to work, teams, leadership, relationships, and change. You will be given the total, undivided attention of the listeners in your group for five minutes. You should share:

    What was the most satisfying work experience you ever had?

    What was the most effective team you were ever on?

    What are you like to work with on a team?

    What are you like as a leader?

    How have you contributed to the nature of the relationships on this team?

    What have you learned about creating change through your experiences?

    What else are you willing to share about yourself?

The role of the listeners

- Give your total, undivided attention to the person sharing
- Just listen, don't interview
- Don't interrupt
- Don't take notes
- Help the person sharing feel comfortable but keep the focus of attention on the person

The role of the feedback givers

- After five minutes has elapsed, please feed back to the sharer:

    What you heard

    What you noticed

    What it meant to you

    What you learned or relearned

tips in exercise 16 just prior to any activity designed to practice key communication skills. Below are some tips on how to provide constructive feedback. I find it useful to remind people that feedback does not mean criticism. Feedback is the loop in a communication process that verifies that a message was received. Team members should describe what they hear before interpreting or evaluating the information shared. To provide constructive feedback, you can:

- Check to see if any feedback is wanted, keeping in mind that timing is crucial
- Describe what you want to feed back without using any words that indicate judgment. Stick to the facts and then check to see if the person you are providing feedback to agrees with your description
- Be specific rather than general
- Indicate what you think the facts mean; provide your interpretation without saying whether you think it is "good" or "bad"
- When you make a judgment statement, praise or criticize the behavior or idea, not the person
- If there is a conflict that is due to differences in values, emphasize the tangible effects of the differences
- Direct the feedback toward things that the receiver can do something about; allow the receiver to suggest changes in behavior before offering options yourself
- If the feedback leads to agreements, summarize who will do what with whom and by when at the end of the conversation
- Remember, feedback does not mean criticisms only

Accepting and Celebrating Differences

Getting team members to share information is crucial to team success, but sometimes it is not what you say that is important but how you say it. How you say something might be okay for someone who has the same personality or background as you, but the message may be lost on others. Teams that have members from different backgrounds and with diverse personalities are potentially better equipped to solve more complicated problems. However, this is an advantage only when people accept differences and look forward to gaining the differing perspectives. Many people have not spent much time figuring out their own personality, let alone the personalities of teammates.

Using Jungian Type Theory

A relatively simple yet powerful framework for understanding personality types was developed by Carl Jung in 1921. It has been simplified and expanded by Isabel Briggs Myers and Katharine Briggs over the last four decades. They have developed an instrument called the *Myers-Briggs Type Indicator®* (MBTI®) that has proven to be a very useful tool for self-awareness and team building. In this section, we will explore the conceptual framework underlying the MBTI instrument and suggest strategies for using the insights it provides to improve relations on a team. For a comprehensive and thorough examination of how to use the MBTI framework for team building, see Sandra Hirsh's (1992) *MBTI Team Building Program: Leader's Resource Guide.*

There are a couple of key points one should know about Jung's original theory of personality types. He suggested that personality traits exist in pairs of opposites. Thus, a person is neither "good" nor "bad" on a given trait but rather favors one side of the trait more than the other. This is why his theory is a "type" rather than a "trait" theory. While traits exist in pairs of opposites, it is important to remember that neither side of the trait is better than the other side. In fact, they complement each other. Each person is said to have a natural or developed preference for one side of the pair over the other, but we all have some portion of each. To illustrate this key point, please try the activity in exercise 18.

Did you notice that you could write your signature with your dominant hand without hardly thinking about it. However, it probably felt awkward to use your nondominant hand. You probably had to concentrate more to use this side of you and it still came across as less well developed. This is Jung's message to us regarding personality type preferences. You will find one side of each trait easier or more natural to utilize. The other side of the trait is also a part of your personality; however, when you use it, it will feel more awkward, you may need to concentrate more to use it, and it will probably still come across as less well developed. Jung did not suggest that you try to develop your ability to use each side equally. Instead, his notion of a well-developed personality is capitalizing on one's preferred characteristics and accepting, even celebrating, teammates/partners who have preferences opposite to one's own. Instead of trying to be all things to all people, it is best to know your personality preferences and provide the strengths of those preferences.

EXERCISE 18

Your Dominant Hand

Directions: Sign your name in the first space provided below; then sign (don't print) your name using your nondominant hand and notice the experience.

_____

_____

In order to communicate and relate to teammates who are different than you, you will need to understand your own personality and make predictions regarding the personalities of the people you want to relate to. In this section, the four key personality traits addressed by the MBTI will be described. You will be asked to make decisions regarding your personality type and the type preferences of your key teammates (or other key people in your life). Review the information provided in tables 11 through 14 as you read through this section. You can then use them to help determine your type and the types of others you work and live with in an exercise later in this chapter (see exercise 19). If you have the opportunity to have the MBTI administered to you by a qualified professional, compare your results with the selections you record in exercise 19. While no instrument is completely reliable or valid, the MBTI is one of the most researched personality type indicators in the world.

Extraversion (E)–Introversion (I)

The first trait of Jung's personality theory and the MBTI framework will be referred to as _life orientation._ Jung labeled the two sides of this trait as Extraversion (E) and Introversion (I). Basically, people with a preference for Extraversion are oriented toward the outer world of people and things, while those with a preference for Introversion are oriented toward the inner world of concepts and ideas. Now look at the two columns of table 11. You will see parts of your personality in both columns. However, one column should provide a clearer description of your natural preferences. Don't choose a column just because it describes characteristics of what you would like to be like. In fact, don't even necessarily choose the column that describes how you actually behave, for sometimes we behave in certain ways to satisfy expectations rather than exhibiting our natural self. Dig deep down and attempt to select the column that overall best describes the real you. Likewise, make predictions regarding your teammates and record your decisions on exercise 19.

Based on the samples provided in the manual for the MBTI (Myers and McCaulley, 1985), our best guess would be that the U.S. population is almost evenly split between people who have a preference for Extraversion and those with a preference for Introversion. Extraverts may feel annoyed by Introverts who might not speak up at team meetings unless they are called on, who act cautious and reluctant to move forward on projects, and who may appear secretive even if they don't mean to be. Many Extraverts feel, Hey, don't get caught up in your shorts. Let's get going on this thing. Meanwhile, Introverts are thinking, Here we go again; we're going to just dive into this mess without really thinking about a plan.

Introverts may be frustrated by the willingness of Extraverts to just wing things. It may just amaze an Introvert that an Extravert is willing to say something without really thinking about it. However, Extraverts need Introverts for planning and depth, and Introverts need Extraverts for action and breadth. It is not enough to merely tolerate these differences—though that is a good start—in order for a team to have great interpersonal relationships. These differences must be celebrated and actively encouraged. When Extraverts can honestly say, "Thank goodness we have these Introverts; they saved us from getting in over our heads!" and when Introverts can say, "Hallelujah, those Extraverts finally got us going on this opportunity and are contacting all those other people that we need some input from!", then the dynamics of diversity will begin to pay big dividends to the team.

Team procedures may need to be adjusted to account for these differences. For example, instead of assuming that everyone is free to speak up if they have something to say on a topic at team meetings, time should be allowed for Introverts to reflect on the issues (ideally in silence) and then organize the discussion by going around the table and asking each member to comment if they wish.

When an Extravert is having some difficulty communicating with an Introverted teammate, she or he might try some of the following strategies:

Table 11 Life Orientation: Extraversion and Introversion

Extraverts	Introverts
Are outwardly directed	Are inwardly directed
Do, consider, do	Consider, do, consider
Think by talking to people	Think a lot before talking
Gain energy by interacting	Discharge energy by interacting with people; need time alone
Are willing to wing it; use trial-and-error learning	Are initially reserved/cautious before acting
Are more accessible; others understand them more	Are known by few; may appear secretive
Have broad interests	Have deep interests
May view things superficially	May appear intense
Are more typically optimistic	Are resistant to generalizations
Are perceptive of external/informal standards	Don't pick up on norms or ignore them
Need isolation to bring out Introversion	Need structure/role to bring out Extraversion
Have relationships with many people; good at starting relationships	Limit relationships; find small talk difficult; find the first step difficult
Focus on the world of people and things	Focus on the world of concepts and ideas
Notice everything; don't mind interruptions much	Hate to be interrupted; are more comfortable with silence
Are willing to share what they think or feel	Tend to wait to be asked things

- Send a note to the Introvert in advance of a meeting to let him or her know what you want to talk about. This will allow the Introvert to collect his or her thoughts
- Focus in on the subject of concern. Do not expect the Introvert to engage in small talk leading up to the conversation. Allow him or her time alone after the conversation if it was lengthy
- Ask questions and then pause without attempting to start answering the question for the person

When Introverts are having some difficulty communicating with an Extraverted teammate, they might try some of the following strategies:

- Warn the Extravert that you might want to just talk about the topic, not necessarily do something about it right away

- Gently remind the Extravert what the topic is. Expect and allow for a broader discussion than what you originally had in mind
- Prepare a list (in your head or on paper) of key things you want to make sure the Extravert hears from you. This is to safeguard against getting so caught up in what the Extravert has to say that you forget to assert your points

Sensing (S)–Intuition (N)

Jung called the second trait of his theory the *perceiving function*. It basically deals with how we come to understand what is going on in the world. Again, he said there are two basic approaches to this function, which he labeled Sensing (S) and Intuition (N). Look over the two columns of table 12 and attempt to determine which side of this trait you prefer to use to understand your world. Record your decision and your predictions of key teammates on exercise 19.

It is great to have some people with a preference for Intuition on a team. People with a preference for Sensing need Intuitives to raise new possibilities and push for complex views, the big picture, and the future. Available samples seem to indicate there are far fewer Intuitives than Sensors in the U.S. population. In fact, in most samples, there are at least twice as many Sensors than Intuitives. It is also great to have some Sensors on your team. Intuitives need Sensors to make ideas more realistic, practical, and factual; attend to details; and focus on the short term. If a team is blessed with both preferences on its roster, it has the potential for greater balance. Just as with any personality difference, the differences in this approach can create conflict. Sensors may roll their eyes and criticize Intuitive teammates for being too idealistic and futuristic, while Intuitives may view Sensors as "stick in the muds" who are tied to the past and do not have a vision of where they should be headed. Celebrating the differences is the key to building better relationships on teams. Don't expect or encourage teammates to be just like yourself. Reap the benefits of complementary styles.

When a Sensor is having some difficulty communicating with an Intuitive teammate, she or he might try some of the following strategies:

- Don't limit your arguments to a solution that will solve a current problem. The Sensor should speculate that this solution might have a further reaching impact and ask the Intuitive to work with him or her to identify the possibilities

Table 12 The Perceiving Function: Sensing and Intuition

Sensors	Intuitives
Are more interested in facts and actualities	Are more interested in possibilities
Attend to details; see the trees better than the forest	Notice the patterns; see the forest better than the trees
Are more patient with routines	Are more patient with complexity
Are sensible/practical/pragmatic; down to earth	Are imaginative/innovative/idealistic; head in clouds
Are present oriented; here-and-now; see what is	Are future oriented; see what could be
Hate to see people making things overly complicated	Enjoy complexity/theories
Are steady workers	Work in bursts
Are systematic and persistent	Jump to conclusions
Mistrust intuition	Ignore some facts
Have/value common sense	Have/value creativity
Are investigators/implementers	Are originators/promoters
Learn through the five senses and by imitating and instruction	Learn by initiating/insight
Are better at responding to what is actually said	Read between the lines
Believe creativity is 99 percent perspiration, 1 percent inspiration	Believe creativity comes in a flash of inspiration
May act like Joe Friday of Dragnet	May act like Isaac Newton with the apple

- If you want to present many facts to the Intuitive, you should suggest to the person that the facts should fit into X (where X is less than the number of facts that will be presented) categories and that the categories may be somewhat related. The Intuitive may then be better prepared to listen to the facts and help sort them into a meaningful pattern that you can both appreciate
- Warn the Intuitive of the dangers of jumping to conclusions. You should make it clear that you believe that the two of you can make sense of the matter if you go over the information thoroughly together

When an Intuitive is having some difficulty communicating with a Sensor teammate, she or he might try some of the following strategies:

- Let the Sensor know that you believe there are practical implications for and applications of the idea you want to present. The Intuitive can either think up some of these possibilities alone or work with the Sensor to discover them
- Provide examples of concepts
- Suggest trial periods for ideas that will require change
- Explain what the first steps would be if the idea were to be put into practice

Thinking (T)–Feeling (F)

The third trait of Jung's personality theory (and the MBTI framework) is referred to as the *judging function*. It focuses on how we come to decisions (making judgments) in our lives. One preference, Thinking (T), describes people who want to keep things as objective as possible and use the principles of logic to arrive at conclusions. They may even apply logic when logic is illogical, say, in making decisions regarding such things as aesthetics, ethics, or values. The other preference on this trait is called Feeling (F). But be careful of this term. Jung is referring to a cognitive function here, so he doesn't mean emotional feeling. Feelers make decisions based on their values and beliefs. We all use logic and we all use our values and beliefs to make decisions. The point is to determine which is your more natural preference when you are faced with a decision. Examine the two columns in table 13 and determine which descriptions seem to match your general tendency. Record your decision and your predictions of key teammates in exercise 19.

This is the only aspect of this personality theory in which there appears to be a systematic sex difference. In the U.S. population, an estimated two-thirds of males prefer Thinking and one-third prefer Feeling, while the ratio is the reverse for females—two-thirds of females prefer the Feeling approach to decision making and one-third prefer the Thinking approach.

On a team, Thinkers need Feelers to persuade others, be sensitive, and establish ethics and values. Feelers need Thinkers to analyze, criticize, and push for consistency. Thinkers may experience Feelers as too concerned with people's feelings and guilty of not confronting issues for fear of offending others. Feelers may experience Thinkers as impersonal and willing to endanger team spirit through their openness to debate and arguments. Together they are more capable of examining problems from a people and a task point of view.

Table 13 The Judging Function: Thinking and Feeling

Thinkers	Feelers
Apply principles of logic to reach conclusions	Apply values and beliefs to reach conclusions
Emphasize an objective/true–false orientation	Emphasize a subjective/agree–disagree orientation
May come across as impersonal without intending to be	Are more naturally friendly unless their values are threatened
Are analytical, skeptical, questioning	Are more trusting; may be overly accepting
Choose truth over tact	Choose tact over truth
Appreciate a good argument	Fear conflict; prize harmony
Feel justice = treating everyone the same	Feel justice = treating everyone separately
Persuade via logic	Persuade via arousal of values and enthusiasm
Are more likely to rationalize their values and beliefs	Clearly know their priorities, beliefs, values
Are more nonchalant about good work (their own and others')	Give and desire appreciation more readily
Are less likely to be sensitive to feelings (their own and others')	Are more likely to be able to predict feelings (their own and others')
Examine consequences from an objective point of view	Examine consequences from a "people" point of view
Are more likely to intellectualize their feelings	Are more likely to subjectively bias their thoughts
Contribute to problem solving by exposing flaws to solutions and by being systematic analysts	Contribute to problem solving by encouraging others and by establishing ethical guidelines for decisions

When a Thinker is having some difficulty communicating with a Feeling teammate, she or he might try some of the following strategies:

- Don't just dive into an argument. Say hello. Ask how things have been going first
- Logically figure out the ethical and "people" implications of the points you want to raise in advance of the conversation. These may be the points of contention. The Thinker can then consider whether there is a way to accommodate the Feeler
- Genuinely express appreciation for contributions the Feeler is making in the conversation or has been making on the team. Praise should not be reserved for extraordinary accomplishments only.

If a Feeler is having some difficulty communicating with a Thinking teammate, she or he might try some of the following strategies:

- Get to the point fairly quickly
- Before the conversation takes place, reflect on what you want to present and identify those elements that you would like accepted on the basis of faith or because they seem to be the right way to go. The Feeler should identify some objective reasons for these beliefs to supplement this point of view
- Do not assume that the lack of an enthusiastic response means rejection of your ideas or of you. Be patient; have faith; try not to fall into righteousness
- Remind the Thinker that no solution to a complex organizational problem can be perfect. Accept criticisms that make sense and attempt to work with the Thinker to come to a conclusion regarding what is the best choice among imperfect options

Judging (J)–Perceiving (P)

The final element of type addressed by the MBTI framework was inferred in Jung's writings but not explicitly part of his typology. We will refer to it as *lifestyle attitude*. The two sides to this trait are Judging (J) and Perceiving (P) and they refer back to the previous two dimensions of the Jungian framework that we just examined. Keep in mind that Judging does not mean judgmental and that Perceiving does not suggest perceptiveness. People with a preference for Judging push for closure. They don't like to leave loose ends and want an orderly approach to things and are quite willing to make decisions to gain this organized approach if no one else is there to do it. People with a preference for Perceiving, on the other hand, want to experience life and understand things. They don't want to miss out on things and are willing to keep things open-ended in case something else comes up. They like to see many options and may be more flexible, but they may also come across as indecisive. In their drive to gain more and more information and options, they may procrastinate decision making too long. Look at the two columns in table 14 and determine which descriptions match your general tendency. Record your decision and your predictions of key teammates in exercise 19.

Table 14 The Lifestyle Attitude: Judging and Perceiving

Judgers	Perceivers
Push for closure	Push for understanding
Keep plugging away until something's finished	Keep things open-ended/hate to miss out on anything
Get greatest pleasure from finishing things	Get greatest pleasure from starting things
Are more decisive/purposeful	Are more flexible/indecisive but better at generating options
May push for decisions too quickly	May procrastinate decisions too much
Prefer plans/order	Prefer a spontaneous approach
Like schedules/to-do lists and try to keep to them	Like to respond to things as they arise
Want things decided in advance and to have expectations clear	Want to keep options open
Are more goal/outcome oriented	Are more process oriented
Want to only know the best way to do things	Want to know all the ways to do things
May rigidly follow plans	May fail to follow through on things
Take deadlines seriously	Use deadlines to get started
May cut off information too quickly to reach a decision	May seek out more information than they need or can use
Prefer their Thinking–Feeling function	Prefer their Sensing–Intuitive function
May feel anxious until a decision is made but then relax because it is made	Are anxious before a decision is made and then prone to second guessing

In the U.S. population, an estimated 60 percent of people have a preference for Judging, while about 40 percent have a preference for Perceiving. Judgers need Perceivers to seek out additional information and to ensure open-mindedness. Teams that push for decisions too quickly often do not reach true consensus and suboptimize their solutions to problems. However, Perceivers need Judgers to push for closure and to keep on plan. Without a clear sense of direction the team cannot be effective for long. Teams must move on to keep up with the dizzying rate of change in today's business world. There is no clear rule for how long decisions should be kept open. The Judgers and the Perceivers on a team need to accept the importance of their conflicting drives. Teams must remain flexible and review sufficient information to make reasonable decisions. However, teams who wait too long

EXERCISE 19

Using Type Preferences to Understand Yourself

Directions: As each of the MBTI preferences is explained, try to predict your type and the type of key people in your work and personal life. Remember, the purpose of using the MBTI framework is to understand similarities and to help celebrate the differences in the people you need to relate to.

Person	Preference (E or I, S or N, T or F, J or P)
1. (you) _____	_____
2. _____	_____
3. _____	_____
4. _____	_____
5. _____	_____
6. _____	_____
7. _____	_____
8. _____	_____
9. _____	_____
10. _____	_____

miss out on opportunities and teams that fluctuate too much lose their sense of identity. Teams blessed with a balance of both Judging and Perceiving members may have the strengths of both preferences.

If a Judger is having some difficulty communicating with a Perceiving teammate, she or he might try some of the following strategies:

■ Gently remind the teammate of the focus you want in the conversation but attempt to hold back some of your own urges to just get it over with

- Suggest that it might be helpful to reach some closure on this issue but that you are open to the fact that this issue might lead to other approaches for other issues
- Jointly choose a deadline for when a decision needs to be made and later diplomatically remind the teammate of the deadline in advance before it arrives

If a Perceiver is having some difficulty communicating with a Judger, she or he might try some of the following strategies:

- Emphasize the need for a high-quality solution to the problem being resolved and justify the search for additional information in light of the goal of quality
- Recognize that time is a limited commodity and that some decisions must be made in order not to lose out on some opportunities
- Work with the Judger to generate a to-do list to clarify the open-ended elements of the issue
- Gently remind the Judger that there are several ways to do things and that one size does not fit all. In order to get things done well, the Perceiver may need to go about things differently than the Judger. Emphasize that the important thing will be to get things done
- Generate a list of options in advance of the conversation but put them in some priority order before speaking with the Judging teammate. You might not have time to get around to discussing all of the options.

In this brief look at how personalities affect communications and interpersonal relationships on teams, we examined only four traits. In addition, we only looked at these dimensions separately. The richness of this theory of personality types comes from the ways these functions combine. Table 15 provides a thumbnail sketch of the sixteen personality types that result when combining the selections you made regarding the four functions of Extraversion–Introversion, Sensing–Intuition, Thinking–Feeling, and Judging–Perceiving. But keep in mind that there are many more traits that make up a personality. This framework does not cover everything to be said about personality, yet there is so much to be said about even these elements. References and resources are provided at the back of this book to enable you to learn more about your own personality and the personalities of your teammates.

Table 15 The Sixteen Types of the *Myers-Briggs Type Indicator*

ISTJ

Serious, quiet, earn success by concentration and thoroughness. Practical, orderly, matter-of-fact, logical, realistic, and dependable. See to it that everything is well organized. Take responsibility. Make up their own minds as to what should be accomplished and work toward it steadily, regardless of protests or distractions.

ISTP

Cool onlookers—quiet, reserved, observing and analyzing life with detached curiosity and unexpected flashes of original humor. Usually interested in cause and effect, how and why mechanical things work, and in organizing facts using logical principles. Excel at getting to the core of a practical problem and finding the solution.

ESTP

Good at on-the-spot problem solving. Like action, enjoy whatever comes along. Tend to like mechanical things and sports. Adaptable, tolerant, pragmatic; focused on getting results. Dislike long explanations. Are best with real things that can be worked, handled, taken apart, or put together.

ESTJ

Practical, realistic, matter-of-fact, with a natural head for business or mechanics. Not interested in abstract theories; want learning to have direct and immediate application. Like to organize and run activities. Often make good administrators; are decisive, quickly move to implement decisions; take care of routine details.

ISFJ

Quiet, friendly, responsible, and conscientious. Work devotedly to meet their obligations. Lend stability to any project or group. Thorough, painstaking, accurate. Their interests are usually not technical. Can be patient with necessary details. Loyal, considerate, perceptive, concerned with how other people feel.

ISFP

Retiring, quietly friendly, sensitive, kind, modest about their abilities. Shun disagreements, do not force their opinions or values on others. Usually do not care to lead but are often loyal followers. Often relaxed about getting things done because they enjoy the present moment and do not want to spoil it by undue haste or exertion.

ESFP

Outgoing, accepting, friendly, enjoy everything and make things more fun for others by their enjoyment. Like action and making things happen. Know what's going on and join in eagerly. Find remembering facts easier than mastering theories. Are best in situations that need sound common sense and practical ability with people.

ESFJ

Warm-hearted, talkative, popular, conscientious, born cooperators, active committee members. Need harmony and may be good at creating it. Always doing something nice for someone. Work best with encouragement and praise. Main interest is in things that directly and visibly affect people's lives.

Table 15 The Sixteen Types of the *Myers-Briggs Type Indicator* continued

INFJ

Succeed by perseverance, originality, and desire to do whatever is needed or wanted. Put their best efforts into their work. Quietly forceful, conscientious, concerned for others. Respected for their firm principles. Likely to be honored and followed for their clear visions as to how best to serve the common good.

INTJ

Have original minds and great drive for their own ideas and purposes. Have long-range vision and quickly find meaningful patterns in external events. In fields that appeal to them, they have a fine power to organize a job and carry it through. Skeptical, critical, independent, determined, have high standards of competence and performance.

INFP

Quiet observers, idealistic, loyal. Important that outer life be congruent with inner values. Curious, quick to see possibilities, often serve as catalysts to implement ideas. Adaptable, flexible, and accepting unless a value is threatened. Want to understand people and ways of fulfilling human potential. Little concern with possessions or surroundings.

INTP

Quiet and reserved. Especially enjoy theoretical or scientific pursuits. Like solving problems with logic and analysis. Interested mainly in ideas, with little liking for parties or small talk. Tend to have sharply defined interests. Need careers where some strong interest can be used and useful.

ENFP

Warmly enthusiastic, high-spirited, ingenious, imaginative. Able to do almost anything that interests them. Quick with a solution for any difficulty and ready to help anyone with a problem. Often rely on their ability to improvise instead of preparing in advance. Can usually find compelling reasons for whatever they want.

ENTP

Quick, ingenious, good at many things. Stimulating company, alert and outspoken. May argue for fun on either side of a question. Resourceful in solving new and challenging problems, but may neglect routine assignments. Apt to turn to one new interest after another. Skillful in finding logical reasons for what they want.

ENFJ

Feel real concern for what others think or want, and try to handle things with due regard for the other's feelings. Can present a proposal or lead a group discussion with ease and tact. Sociable, popular, sympathetic. Responsive to praise and criticism. Like to facilitate others and enable people to achieve their potential.

ENTJ

Frank, decisive, leaders in activities. Develop and implement comprehensive systems to solve organizational problems. Good in anything that requires reasoning and intelligent talk, such as public speaking. Are usually well informed and enjoy adding to their fund of knowledge.

Resolving Conflict Constructively

Conflict is a natural and daily phenomenon on teams. But conflict needn't be nasty. Conflict is merely the result of having the benefit of people with different perspectives on a team. It is, however, a powerful force and must be handled constructively. Thus, conflict has certain advantages and disadvantages. Some potential advantages include that:

- It is a prerequisite to change.
- It indicates caring.
- It generates energy (anti-apathy).
- External conflict usually results in internal cohesion.
- The expression of conflict can be cathartic and reduce tension.

Some of the potential disadvantages of conflict are that:

- It can result in polarization.
- It disrupts other productive activity.
- It can encourage the use of politics and emotions and reduce the use of reason and logic.

According to Thomas and Kilmann (1974), there are basically five ways to deal with conflict, which they call Avoiding, Accomodating, Competing, Compromising, and Collaborating. Each approach has its own potential advantages and drawbacks, if used too frequently.

Avoiding

Sometimes it is best to just avoid a potential conflict situation with a teammate. Occasionally we should pretend we didn't hear what she or he said, deny that anything is bothering us, withdraw from the situation, look the other way, or repress or let go of memories of past transgressions. The best times to use avoiding is when an issue is very unimportant or when there is very little chance that you would "win" the argument and going for the bait may be dangerous for your situation or for the team. Some of the potential advantages of the avoiding approach are that the conflict may go away, there may be less stress, and for survival considerations. Some of the potential disadvantages of this approach are that the problem will not be resolved, the problem may grow into a bigger one, and it may generate doubts in oneself or one's organization.

Accommodating

Sometimes it might be better to acknowledge that a potential conflict exists but not engage in pursuing what is right for the situation. You might just give in to what your teammate wants, or maybe smooth over the situation, letting the teammate know that you recognize the person's feelings about the situation and that your relationship with the teammate is more important than the issue. Sometimes you can try to defuse the situation by putting the issue into a broader perspective or by using humor to reduce tensions. Sometimes you should just say that if you talk about it now, you might say something you might regret later. If that is the case, then ask for a time when you can get back together to discuss the issue. Use the accommodating approach whenever the relationship is clearly more important than the issue, you are clearly wrong and need to admit it, you need to save your strength and "points" for bigger issues that you anticipate will be coming up, and you want to show that you can be reasonable. Some potential advantages of this approach are that it allows you to show concern for the relationship and buys you time so that cooler heads can prevail when you deal with the issue later. Some of the potential disadvantages of this approach are that one or both parties usually do not get back together to resolve the problem, only a small part of the problem gets resolved, it generates doubts and fears over when the issue comes up again, and it can earn you a reputation of not being a "straight shooter."

Competing

Sometimes you should engage in a discussion and attempt to convince your teammate (or teammates) that your position is right. This might involve eventually putting the issue up to a vote and allowing the majority to rule. This approach could also be a matter of asserting your authority if that is relevant to the issue or bouncing the decision up the chain of command for someone else to decide. The best time to use this approach is when time is of the essence, for example, in an emergency or when there is a deadline that must be met. Some of the potential advantages to this approach are that it helps get the issue settled, can save some time, and allows the "winners" to feel good about the decision. Some of the potential disadvantages of this approach are that it creates "losers" and those who feel they've lost may try to get even through rebelling, fighting future issues, or withdrawing; it encourages polarization, causing people to ask, "Whose side are you on?"; and it creates a political culture in the organization.

Compromising

Sometimes you ought to try to split the difference with a teammate by meeting the person half-way on the issue. Find the average difference between your points of view—the middle ground. This approach may be best used when the issue is somewhat important but not really worth disrupting the team's dynamics, which would occur if a more confrontive approach were used. This might also be useful if the team members have to principally satisfy people outside of the team and the team is of secondary importance to all of the members. Some of the potential advantages of this approach are that it demonstrates concern for whether the other party will also "look good," builds the belief that the other party is willing to work with you, enables both parties to get something, and enables issues to get settled. Some of the potential disadvantages of this approach are that the solution may not settle the problem and both sides may lose, the solutions tend to get "watered down," and it sets up the game of "low ball/high ball" of initial offers that lead to distrust.

Collaborating

The most difficult but potentially most rewarding approach to con- flict resolution is the collaborative approach. This is basically creative problem solving. It is an attempt to discover solutions that integrate and build on the perspectives of the parties engaged in the conflict. It is the search for the so-called "win–win" solution. It is important to engage in this approach because it builds teams. It simultaneously shows concern for task and for relationships. It is the embodiment of the notion that the team approach is a superior way of making deci- sions. Some of the potential advantages to this approach are that it encourages higher quality decisions and more innovative solutions, allows both parties to fully win and feel good, reduces the fear of future conflict, and builds respect for the other party. Some of the potential disadvantages of this approach are that it is very time consuming, it is essential for both parties to be skilled at using the approach, and it is necessary for both parties to be willing to use this approach.

In order to use this approach, the discussion of the issue must be initiated diplomatically. Whoever brings the issue up needs to focus on the facts and the tangible effects of the potential conflict on the parties involved. It is important that when an issue is discussed there is no attacking, demeaning, or discounting of the other party, especially during the opening of the discussion. Both parties need to choose their words carefully to find a way to reduce the need for defensiveness. It will not help to debate value differences, as adults rarely change their values through engaging in rational discussions. It is more important that the parties look for a mutual interest that could be achieved if resolution is reached. Basically, following the steps of the 4-A problem-solving model discussed in chapter 7 will provide a process for reaching a collaborative resolution. Both parties must practice their best listening and feedback skills. Establishing ground rules for the discussion will also help. The four principles of the win–win approach have been stated as:

1. Focus on the issues, not the personalities
2. Focus on issues, not positions
3. Generate options to satisfy mutual interests
4. Utilize external standards to judge the options

In *Getting To Yes,* Fisher and Ury (1981) provide readers with an excellent guide for applying these principles.

Dealing With Particularly Difficult People

The five approaches to dealing with conflict described in the previous section should help you resolve issues with just about everyone. However, aren't there some people on teams or in your personal life who are particularly difficult to deal with? People who take on the characteristics of the know-it-all, the grudge holder, the noncommunicator, the person who gets angry easily, the guilt tripper, the politician, the liar, the intimidator, and the clown.

Your usual methods of dealing with conflict will not work with such people. You have to first decide if it is worth dealing with this person (because of the task, because of the relationship). You probably will not change them, but you can change how you react to them. If you are willing to try dealing with them at least one more time, I recommend following the seven steps outlined below.

1. *Prepare for the confrontation.* Observe the person for about a week. Note the person's patterns, especially what she or he tends to say. Pay

attention to what the person actually says or does. Try to remove your preconceived notions about him or her. Treat the person as though she or he is a scientific experiment and you are trying to document an objective pattern instead of trying to catch them doing something wrong. Also prepare a time or two that you are willing to work with this person on the conflict situation and get clear in your own mind why you want to work out things with this person.

2. *Initiate the confrontation by stating what impact the conflict is having on the situation.* Choose a time and a place where the person will not have to save face in front of anyone else. Do not attack, discount, or demean the person. Do not begin by stating your position or what you want as a solution to the problem. Instead, describe the circumstances and why you honestly want to build a relationship with this person that works. Point out any tangible effects that the conflict between the two of you may be causing.

3. *Whatever the person says after your opening comments, repeat back to them their own words.* Practice your best descriptive listening skills in a nonmocking manner. This will allow the person to hear themselves and perhaps take back some of what she or he has been saying, thus opening the door for negotiating a better relationship. At the very least, it will give the person some attention, and that is just what some difficult people want. It will also provide the first set of facts that the two of you can verify and set a tone for the need to clarify assumptions. If the person makes a broad, general accusation of you, repeat back what the accusation is and the implications that it holds for you.

4. *Clarify what the real problem is.* Separate what the root problem is from the symptoms. Do not argue about value differences. Adults do not change their values through debates. Focus the conversation on the problem, its root causes, and the tangible effects of the problem on you, the person, and the other people involved. Be patient. Do not enter into a discussion about who is at fault for things. Push to gain agreement on what the problem is. Make it clear to the person that you want to focus the discussion on *what*, not *who*.

5. *Do not chase or badger.* If the person refuses to discuss what the problem is and walks away, say loudly, ***"I want to work this problem out. It is important to me. I will see you at 3 o'clock tomorrow to see if you want to talk about it then."*** Then make sure you go see the person at whatever time you state. If they again refuse to discuss the

matter, ask them when would be a good time for them to discuss it. If they still refuse, move on to step 7.

6. *Identify no fewer than three options to resolve the problem.* Do not believe that your solution is the only way. Do not believe that you are forced to either give in and agree with the person or fight back. Every problem is caused by many things and there are many solutions to every problem. Perhaps the toughest mental discipline you need to solve a difficult conflict is the need to use creativity to find a solution. Don't fall into the trap of generating all of the options yourself. It just lets the other person pick out the flaws in whatever you come up with. Difficult problems do not have perfect solutions. The only way you and this other person are going to resolve your conflict is if you agree to an imperfect solution together. If there is only one solution being debated, then the two of you will compete over whether it is right or wrong. If there are only two solutions being debated, then the two of you will compete over whose solution is better. Or if two solutions are offered, there will be the temptation to split the difference and call it a compromise. This might work, but usually both sides will believe that the other side padded their offer and the resulting solution may be inadequate and not a source on which to build a trusting relationship. When three or more viable options are being discussed, it is hard to take sides. Insist that the other person generate solutions and be sure to do so yourself. You may have to postpone the discussion until the two of you have had time to think up some options. Make sure that it is clear when the two of you will get back together to discuss the options and that there is agreement that both of you will develop many options.

7. *If all else fails, state what your goals are and express a willingness to negotiate how these goals will be reached.* Be very clear about what you want as an outcome. State it clearly and ask the person if she or he needs any further explanation of what your goals are. At this stage, repeat back to them virtually anything that she or he said and then repeat your goals and your willingness to negotiate how to achieve these goals. Be assertive rather than aggressive. If this does not work, state the consequences for failing to achieve the goals. Try to not make it sound like a threat, but be very clear. Make sure you follow through on anything you say. If the person does change his or her behavior, make sure you praise any improvements (probably in private). If the person interferes with the goals being reached, apply

the consequence and recognize that this is likely to end the relationship. You may have to repeat any agreements made, and this may rekindle an argument. Just be clear on the goals, your willingness to negotiate how the goals are to be met, and any consequences that will occur if the changes do not occur. Follow through very consistently, but don't be a nag. Consistency is the absolute key to rebuilding trust between any two people, even if they are enemies.

Summary

In order for teams to be effective, they must develop and maintain constructive interpersonal relationships. This is a very complex task and entire books have been devoted to this component of effective teams alone. This chapter emphasized that team members must deliver key attitudes (trust, respect, acceptance), key understandings (of the personalities, of self and others) and key skills (communication skills—sharing information, listening effectively, and providing constructive feedback—and conflict resolution skills). We can never achieve perfect relationships. Teams that are hoping for long-term success will need to come back to this component again and again. Continual improvement efforts on this dimension do not have to be approached with a dreadful, serious demeanor. Improving relationships can be fun and exciting, even when it is hard work. Perhaps the most important thing is to attempt to ensure that the steps forward outnumber the steps backward. After making progress in a relationship, there is still a great likelihood that people will slip back into habits that produce problems between teammates. Be very clear with each other about what commitments you are making. Make small promises that you can keep. Make visible signs of keeping promises. Confront "slipups," but let go of the resentments they produce. It is possible to have long-term constructive relationships between teammates, but it takes time, effort, and willingness.

CHAPTER 9

Active Reinforcement Systems

Teams go through various stages of development. Tuckman and Jensen (1977) refer to these stages as forming, norming, storming, producing, and closing. During the *forming stage* members get acquainted with each other and the task they are to accomplish. It is typically a very polite stage in which people are willing to go along with ideas unless someone suggests something that appears to be too radical. People attempt to avoid making any enemies and generally show patience and tolerance as best they can. Eventually, this wears off for some and a certain level of competition for leadership emerges. Key players emerge who seemingly want to influence the approach to the task or have some desire to deal with conflicts they are experiencing with some other members. The result of this *storming stage* is either a united group that is ready to get its act together or a split group, with some people withdrawing from taking on active responsibilities. During the *norming stage,* efforts are made to determine what standards of performance are acceptable: Do we really expect an emphasis on quality? Do we really mean what we say when we set deadlines? Is it okay to miss meetings? Whenever the organization expects some productivity, the group will have to make an effort to deliver it. If they have successfully worked through the forming, storming, and norming stages, they will be a high-performing group. But how long will this last? B. F. Skinner told us long ago that behavior that is positively reinforced will be repeated and behavior that is ignored or punished will be reduced or eliminated.

Individually Based Recognition
for Team-Oriented Behavior

Few organizations have a system for rewarding team-oriented behaviors. The results generated by teams are not directly rewarded nor are the behaviors that made the team satisfying and effective typically recognized. No wonder so many teams get stuck. Behavior is a function of consequences. Some organizations are good at identifying when people are doing things wrong. This can stop some people from taking advantage of a situation, but if there aren't sufficient rewards for doing things "right," it often becomes a "catch me if you can" system with people wondering, What's in it for me?

If you and your team (or teams) are waiting for the organization to reward team-oriented behaviors, you may have a long wait ahead of you. Later in this chapter, we will examine some team-based and organizationally based reward systems that can help reinforce a team-based change effort, but few organizations have developed such systems. The trend is growing, but, in the meantime, I suggest that the key to reinforcing team-oriented behaviors is to get team members to express appreciation to each other. Dubrin (1982) lists many examples of recognition and feels the forms it takes may be almost unlimited. For example, he suggests the following can all reinforce recognition:

- Feedback on behavior
- Praise and encouragement
- Comradeship
- Job security
- Favorable performance appraisals
- Access to confidential information
- Freedom to choose one's work assignments
- Seeing the results of one's own work
- Hearing directly from the consumers of one's work
- Requests for ideas beyond the scope of one's current assignments
- Improved working conditions
- Capable and friendly co-workers
- Business luncheons
- Time off from work
- Status symbols or awards

I have worked with many teams in which a decision was made that every third or fourth meeting (or approximately once a month) an agenda item was established for the expressed purpose of recognizing teammates who had contributed to the effectiveness and/or satisfaction level of the team. I don't recommend establishing a "team player of the month." This generally breeds some competition or resentment. Instead, use the time allocated to recognize as many individuals as possible for specific acts of contribution.

If it has been a long time since such recognition has taken place (or if it never has), a whole session could be dedicated to this purpose. Each individual can be spotlighted for three to five minutes. The employee is asked to clarify his or her personal commitments to helping the team become more effective and satisfying and is then showered with positive but genuine feedback from teammates. Small contributions that supported team processes should be recognized as well as any major accomplishments that have boosted the team's outcomes. Comments such as "Thanks for always coming prepared to team meetings!"; "I appreciate your sunny disposition!"; and "John set a record for units produced per hour last month, which combined with everyone else's performance, ensured that our main customer received their complete order on time!" are the types of comments that are useful and reinforcing. Time needs to be set aside to get each member to publicly state what she or he is willing to commit to do to help the team in its efforts to enhance its effectiveness. But time also needs to be set aside for members to hear from their teammates about what they appreciate. Although it may feel awkward, people need feedback regarding how they have contributed to the work of a team. Exercise 20 provides a set of instructions for conducting such a session.

Behaviors that are not recognized become extinguished. For example, if no one says anything about people showing up on time for team meetings, eventually, someone will show up late. If you want a certain pattern of behavior to exist, say something about it to reinforce it. Do not assume that ordinary actions and courtesies can be counted on. Do not reserve praise only for results or extraordinary contributions to team processes. Find a way to ensure that time is devoted to teammates expressing appreciation to other teammates. Tubbs (1994) suggests that there are four basic categories of recognition that you can provide: (1) interpersonal (e.g., acknowledgment

EXERCISE 20

Contributing to the Work Group

Directions: You have undoubtedly discussed many issues and plans together as a team. There will always be more things that need to be done in order for your team to be an excellent team and maintain its effectiveness. In this exercise, each team member should take a turn in the "hot seat" to state his or her commitment to the team and to receive feedback from your teammates as to why they are glad that you are on this team. Thus, when it is your turn:

Give a statement regarding:

How will you contribute to the work that still needs to be accomplished? Clarify the commitments that you are willing to make to your teammates. How will you help this group accomplish what it now believes needs to be accomplished? What will you do? By when? The more specific you are, the more likely you will follow through on your promises.

Receive the feedback on:

What do your teammates think you have done that has positively contributed to their working together as a team?

Your teammates are to provide you with positive feedback regarding how they have seen you contribute to the work of this group in the past, especially recently.

of existence, showing concern, saying hello), (2) task (e.g., empowering individuals and enriching the tasks to demonstrate belief in the abilities and responsibility levels of the team members), (3) status-related (e.g., titles, power, opportunities for training), and (4) financial recognition, which Stack (1992) and others suggest is the ultimate form of recognition in a business setting and that the challenge for leadership is to find ways to provide for this.

Individuals do not typically receive financial rewards for being team oriented when the team only engages in problem-solving activities and/or offers recommendations of what should be done to improve a work process. However, one of the more common forms of financial rewards provided to team members during the establishment of self-directed work teams is a pay-for-knowledge/skills system. As a member takes on more responsibility for his or her current job assignment (e.g., maintaining a machine as well as operating it), learns how to perform the jobs of other team members, or develops and takes on leadership and other administrative responsibilities, the person receives an increase in pay. Team members are expected to assist in cross-training and the organization must provide time and other assistance for the acquisition of the knowledge and skills. Since the member is now more "valuable" to the organization, compensation should be provided.

There needs to be some certification process to verify that the member truly can perform the additional duties. Agreements regarding the rotation of assignments should be worked out in advance. At one organization that I am familiar with, team members were empowered to determine when teammates understood each other's job. The teammate then received an additional 25¢ per hour for every additional job learned and then an additional 50¢ per hour after she or he knew all the jobs of the team. After four months, all team members were declared knowledgeable of all jobs and became the highest paid employees in the plant. However, no rotation of job duties was taking place. Management wanted greater flexibility and wanted to eventually eliminate the need for any relief workers. They began to question the certification process performed by the workforce. The workers suspected that management was using the cross-training system to eliminate even more jobs on the team. The suspicions led to the demise of the team concept at that location. A pay-for-skill system can be beneficial for all parties involved but careful planning and agreements must be established in advance.

Group-Based Approaches to Team Rewards

Organizations are beginning to establish incentive plans to reward teams for their accomplishments. Most efforts are extensions of incentive plans that were originally designed to reward individuals. In this system, the team, instead of an individual, receives a reward for a suggestion or for exceeding a production standard. Sometimes the reward is monetary, with the team deciding how to split up the award. More often, the reward is symbolic. At one plant I know, whenever a team exceeds its monthly quality and production standards, management cooks and serves a lunch or dinner for the team members. Other examples of team rewards include increases in the team's training budget; hats, jackets, and shirts; publicity via pictures, banners, and articles in the company newsletter; recognition at all-employee meetings for the team's accomplishments; tickets to sporting events; and special parking privileges. Reactions to team-based reward systems have thus far been mixed. Sometimes members revel in the recognition for the group's accomplishment. Sometimes the reward focuses concern on the slackers who receive the same reward but didn't really contribute equitably toward the goal. Team-based reward systems can encourage competition between groups, which can lead to less cooperative behavior and can hurt the overall organization. I have witnessed examples of teams hoarding parts and tools so that other teams wouldn't surpass them. Anytime an award is based on a judgment of which teams are doing "better" than other teams, as opposed to providing the allowance that all teams that exceed their goals gain some reward or recognition, someone is going to feel resentful. Either some team will be jealous of another team or some group of employees may harass the "winning" teams, accusing them of sucking up to management.

Management must learn not to play one team against another if it hopes to have long-term and widespread success with group-based organizational development interventions. Teams should compete against targets, not each other. French and Hollmann (1975) and others have long advocated a team-based approach to a management-by-objectives (MBO) system. They have pointed out the deficiencies of individually based MBO systems, which include failure to recognize the interdependent nature of most jobs, failure to adequately coordinate the various individual objectives for the benefit of the organization, and failure to use the MBO approach to improve relations. They propose a nine-phase strategy for collaborative MBO (CMBO). French and Hollmann have concluded that the "essential process is one of overlapping work units interacting with 'higher' and 'lower' units on overall organizational goals and objectives, unit goals and objectives, and individuals interacting with peers and superiors on role definition and individual goals and objectives" (p. 18). Table 16 outlines the nine phases of the CMBO system.

Table 16 The Nine Phases of the CMBO System

Phase 1. Diagnosis of organizational problems: Diagnosis is collaboratively conducted by a cross-section of organization members.

Phase 2. Information and dialogue: Workshops on the basic purposes and techniques of CMBO are cascaded down the chain of command, eventually using top- and middle-level managers to conduct these workshops at some point in the chain.

Phase 3. Diagnosis of organizational readiness: Interviews are conducted to verify interest in the willingness to use the CMBO approach. There must be support from the top and interest from overlapping, not scattered, portions of the organization to get started.

Phase 4. Goal setting at the overall organization level: Goals and objectives for a given time period are defined by a team of top-level executives through consensus decision making, though input is solicited from middle- and lower-level employees, too.

Phase 5. Goal setting at the unit level: Teams gather together to identify goals for their own units that would support the accomplishment of the overall organization goals. This is still an interactive process, with input from units higher and lower in the hierarchy, too.

Phase 6. Goal setting at the individual level: Each manager identifies what she or he would need to accomplish in order for the organization to achieve the overall and unit-level objectives. This is done in a session that identifies the responsibilities of all team members and may require time dedicated to role clarification procedures like those explained in Chapter 6.

Phase 7. Performance review: Ongoing discussions between team leaders and managers and team members of the progress being made regarding the objectives are held and also scheduled into team meetings on a regular basis. The leader is responsible for a report at the end of the agreed-upon time period documenting the accomplishments. Discussion of the report includes an emphasis on learning what helped and what hindered the attainment of objectives.

Phase 8. Rediagnosis: A reexamination is undertaken regarding whether CMBO is really helping and what can be done to improve its use if it is to be continued.

Phase 9. Recycle: If the process is continued, Phases 1 through 8 are repeated on at least an annual basis, allowing for ongoing adjustments to the goals and objectives and processes of the CMBO system as needed.

Organizational-Level Rewards for Team-Based Approaches

When an organization is using teams, committees, and task forces to identify problems and recommend solutions that can make a difference, individual-level and group-based recognition and reward processes should be sufficient enough to sustain interest for at least a few years.

However, if the organization is dedicated to using self-directed work teams as a long-term business strategy and structure, a systemwide reward process will be needed. Two approaches will be discussed in this section: (1) revamping the organization's performance appraisal system to recognize the expectation of being team oriented and include all levels of employees in the performance review procedures and (2) establishing a gainsharing plan to provide a structure for teams to participate in cross-functional decision making and share the financial rewards gained by improvements made in the overall effectiveness levels of the organization.

Performance Appraisal Systems in Team-Based Organizations

In order for teams to become increasingly more effective, they need to know how they are doing. In sports, we provide a scoreboard. At work, a feedback system is also needed. Teams need to know if they are winning (accomplishing their objectives), and they need to know how well they are working together (feedback on group processes). In sports, coaches, referees, and fans let the team know when they have scored and when they have run a play well. At work, information on the perceptions of management and customers—internal and external—needs to be made directly available to all team members. In addition, members need to develop enough of a perspective on the business to self-monitor effectiveness and efficiency, especially if there is an attempt to move toward a self-directed workforce. If we are going to take teams seriously, the performance appraisal system for all levels of the organization must include feedback on, and incentives for, the degree to which actions are reinforcing the team approach.

Typically, only managers and some staff receive performance reviews. Most performance appraisal systems have problems that lead to complaints and dissatisfaction. Evaluation criteria for appraisals are often poorly defined, compliance behavior and other cooperative personality traits are generally given too much consideration, company politics influence ratings, and the techniques and paperwork involved may be so cumbersome that managers may just want to get it done rather than do it well.

Many of the problems associated with performance reviews stem from inadequacies in the raters themselves. Few companies provide training for their evaluators, who are prone to all kinds of perceptual errors such as halo effect, projection, and stereotyping. Each supervisor seems to define the standards of performance differently. With one supervisor, several employees may receive "outstanding" ratings, while most of the other employees are described as "very good" or "distinctly above average." Yet another supervisor in the same company may see all employees as average and very rarely provide higher ratings.

Most supervisors, however, fear dealing with conflict over the ratings if they know they will have to provide a face-to-face feedback session. So they either give almost everyone the same rating or are lenient in their evaluations, unless they are evaluating a particularly troublesome or incompetent individual.

Even if a manager is not prone to these rating errors, it is just humanly difficult to be consistent in applying criteria to performances of several individuals, who may have very different or even unequal job assignments. Should you give someone a high rating for doing simple tasks well and a lower rating to someone who is trying as hard or harder as that person but who is assigned to a more difficult set of responsibilities? Too often, the emphasis is placed on judging the performance rather than using the performance review as an opportunity for feedback that would lead to growth and development of talent as well as relationships.

An organization that wants to build effective teams must train those responsible to conduct performance reviews effectively. The system must include criteria relevant to behaviors that encourage a team approach to work. If the system only emphasizes how many parts are getting produced, the motivation will be toward getting short-term results, with little concern for dedicating the time needed to nurture and encourage teamwork. The review must include a look at task accomplishment but should provide an equal weighting for team-building activities and processes at least during the first couple of years that it takes to establish fully functioning work teams.

If the organization is serious about establishing self-directed work teams, team members need to be given the opportunity and responsibility to provide performance feedback to each other and to the leaders and managers assigned to coach them to success. There needs to be a group-level review of the collective accomplishments and shortcomings of the team and then an examination of each individual's contributions. The emphasis should be developmental rather than judgmental.

The session should begin with an effort to confirm whether what the individual's perceptions of what she or he is responsible for is parallel with what the team and other levels of the hierarchy expect. The role clarification procedures described back in chapter 6 can be abridged and serve as a design for the beginning portion of this session. The team member should also be given the opportunity to first rate his or her own behavior and performance. This helps make sure that a range of activities that the job holder believes are relevant to the duties and responsibilities of a team member are examined. It also provides a chance to acknowledge current deficiencies rather than set up peers to act like a panel from the Spanish Inquisition. All parties should be encouraged to begin their statements using descriptive terms and documented facts. Not much time should be spent on establishing a global evaluation along the lines of, "You are a real good teammate." The tips on providing effective feedback contained in chapter 8 should be reviewed and practiced. The genuine strengths of each individual teammate should be emphasized. At no time should a member be asked to work on more than two or three weaknesses at a time, unless there is an intention of removing the member. The purpose of the session is not to identify every mistake anyone has made on the team but rather to focus people on the two or three things that could be done to get the team to its next level of effectiveness. The performance review session could be followed by a mutual goal-setting session. The CMBO approach described earlier in this chapter could serve as a model.

Gainsharing Plans as Rewards in a Team-Based Organization

If the purpose of an organization is to make a profit, then the use of a team approach should be a conscious strategy to enhance efforts to fulfill this purpose. While at first it may feel rewarding enough to learn new things and to be able to have more control and influence over one's work life, eventually teams will want to have a share of the profit generated by their hard work. Profit-sharing plans generate excitement once a year and may encourage longer term employee loyalty. However, it is difficult to form a connection between a team's performance at any given point in time and yearly profit figures. Financial incentives tied to the accomplishment of pre-agreed upon objectives may produce some motivation and satisfaction, but they can lead to a lack of concern for cooperation between teams and the setting of suboptimal goals. Gainsharing plans such as Scanlon Plans, Rucker Plans, and Improshare Plans establish teams as the basic unit of an organization's structure and provide monthly feedback and financial rewards for improvements in overall organizational effectiveness. Although it is beyond the scope of this book to provide a detailed explanation of these organizational development interventions, a short summary will be provided. Interested readers seeking a more in-depth examination might find *Productivity Gainsharing* by Brian Graham-Moore and Timothy Ross (1983) insightful.

Every gainsharing plan must be tailored to the characteristics of the given organization. However, the general thrust of these plans involves establishing a problem-solving team, often called a Departmental Committee, in each work area. The members of this team are representatives and are expected to seek out the suggestions of all of the employees of their area. They help people write up the suggestions, then they review and implement the suggestions they believe make good business sense. If a suggestion would require resources or authority beyond the scope of their team, they present the suggestion to a higher authority for approval. One representative from each Departmental Committee is elected to serve on a top-level Screening Committee that also includes top leadership not associated with a particular work area. Table 17 describes the typical membership and responsibilities of the Screening and Departmental Committees.

Each month, members of the Screening Committee then review the figures associated with the bonus calculations. The bonus formula essentially attempts to reward organizational performance that exceeds expectations. It is based on a ratio of value of goods produced and/or services rendered compared to the cost of labor. Rules are established in advance regarding subtractions that would affect the quantification of value and costs. A given month's ratio is compared with a standard that is usually the historical average for the company over the last three to seven years. The time frame for this process varies with the circumstances of the company. Calculations for five of the more typical bonus formulas associated with gainsharing plans are described below.

Five Gainsharing Formulas

Single Ratio (Scanlon) Formula.   With this formula, the base ratio equals payroll costs divided by net sales. To use this formula, calculate the sales value of production for a given bonus period. Then subtract out the value of any sales returns, allowances, and discounts for the period. Add in the cost, or selling price, of any increase in inventory.

Table 17 Suggestions for Gainsharing Plan Committee Structure

Top-Level Committee (Screening or Steering Committee)

Basic purpose

To represent all major constituencies and provide leadership

Typical membership

Top management

Top union leadership

Financial manager

Human resources manager

Engineer

Supervisor (elected by peers)

Some union committee members or stewards

One representative from each "department"

Responsibilities

Review organizational performance

Review bonus statement thoroughly

Communicate what and why of bonus to others

Final review of suggestions

Sounding board for organizational plans

Decide election and participation rules

Discuss/adjust bonus formula changes

Production Committees (Departmental Committees)

Basic purpose

To solicit participation in problem solving and review suggestions

Typical membership

Supervisor

Steward

Set percentage of the employees in that department

Invited guests/experts

Responsibilities

Solicit identification of problems

Solicit analysis of problems

Solicit options to solve problems

Help people write up suggestions

Review suggestions (standard approach)

Make decisions within their authority

Prepare reports for top-level committee

Develop implementation plans

This represents the value of production. Now multiply this figure by the historically determined ratio between labor costs and sales. The bonus pool will be the resulting "allowed" payroll costs minus the actual payroll costs. The bonus pool is distributed according to previous agreements. Typically, the company gets a certain portion; another portion is put in reserve for deficit months; the remainder is distributed to the participating employees as a percentage of their base pay.

Split Ratio Formula. With this formula, the base ratio equals payroll costs by product or service divided by net sales. To use this formula, calculate the sum of the single ratios for each product or service with the base ratio to determine allowed labor costs established separately for each product or service.

Value-Added (Rucker) Formula. With this formula, the base ratio equals labor costs divided by the value added by labor. To use this formula, calculate the value of production by determining the sales value plus or minus various adjustments such as discounts and returns. Now subtract out the costs of materials, supplies, energy, and any other agreed-upon outside purchases to determine the value added by labor. This figure is then multiplied by the historically determined ratio to establish the allowed employee costs. The bonus pool is the actual (labor) employee costs subtracted from the allowed employee cost figure. The distribution of the pool is determined by prior agreement. Typically, the company gets a portion; a certain portion is put in reserve for deficit periods; and the remainder is distributed to participating employees as a percentage of their base pay.

Multicost Split Ratio Formula. With this formula, the base ratio equals labor plus materials plus overhead all calculated by department and product divided by the sales value of production. To use this formula, calculate the value of production by determining the value of sales plus or minus the value of such things as inventory and allowances. This figure is then multiplied by the historically determined ratio in order to establish the allowable expenses figure. The actual expenses can be calculated by adding together labor costs plus the costs of materials and supplies plus all other agreed-upon expenses, for example, energy. These figures can be calculated by department or product line and then combined. The bonus pool is the difference between the allowable expenses and the actual expenses. The pool is then distributed in a manner similar to the other plans.

Improshare. With this formula, the base ratio equals actual hours divided by the total standard value hours. To use this formula, calculate the work hour standard by dividing the total production hours worked by the number of units produced. Then multiply this by the number of units produced by product line. The base productivity factor (BPF) is then calculated by dividing the total production and "nonproduction" hours by the total standard value hours. The bonus pool is determined by dividing one-half the number of "gained hours" (i.e., the total standard hours for actual units produced less the number of actual hours produced) by the actual hours.

Gainsharing plans use teams as their base and reinforce working together across teams in order for the whole organization to succeed. If the system is used to blame one group or another for failure to gain a bonus in a given month, the plan will not succeed. The track record for gainsharing plans is especially good for moderate-sized companies. In their classic book on gainsharing plans, Frost, Wakeley, and Ruh (1974) suggest that there are four key principles or conditions for successful implementation of gainsharing plans—identity, equity, participation/accountability, and managerial and leadership competence—and define these principles as follows:

- *Identity.* This is the extent to which employees are meaningfully informed of the organization's history, competition, customers, objectives, and so forth. This creates a sense of identification and ownership of the current compelling need for improvement and the development and use of the knowledge of all employees as resources.
- *Equity.* This is the opportunity for all employees to realize an equitable return for increasing the investment of their resources of ideas, energy, competence, and commitment.
- *Participation/accountability.* This is the structured and guaranteed opportunity and responsibility provided to all employees to influence the decision process within the company and to become accurately informed and responsible in their respective areas and roles of competence.
- *Managerial and leadership competence.* This is the inescapable necessity for management and union leadership itself to establish, grow, and develop increasing professional competence and systems with assured participation from all elements of the organization's human resources by gaining commitment rather than merely forcing compliance.

Summary

In order for teams to be effective in the long run, team-oriented behaviors need to be reinforced. Individuals need to be recognized for their contributions. Team members need to understand how effective their collective efforts really are. For there to be results and improvements in the processes, feedback and rewards need to be provided. If teams are to be taken as a serious business strategy, they must have an impact on overall organizational effectiveness. Eventually, an organization must "put its money where its mouth is" if it wants employees to believe that it is making serious efforts to build effective teams. All rewards, financial bonuses as well as improvements in job security and symbolic recognition gestures, should be provided through a system that not only reinforces team effectiveness and satisfaction but also encourages collaboration across teams. Strategies for enhancing relationships across teams are discussed in the next chapter.

CHAPTER 10

Constructive External Relationships

E stablishing and working through internal procedures and relationships are not by themselves enough. Effective teams must also build good relationships with other teams and key players of the organization who are not members. I have seen employee involvement (EI) teams get their own act together and then wonder why the employees from, say, the Maintenance Department dislike them and take forever to respond to their requests for help. In one case I know of, the EI teams had doubled the work load of the Maintenance Department but didn't realize it. All the good ideas they had come up with during their problem-solving sessions required the help of those in the skilled trades and maintenance. During the EI team's presentation to management, they documented how the machines in their department had been neglected. Without fully realizing it, they had made the Maintenance Department look bad and then needed their help to get things done. Well, Maintenance showed them. The EI team members were labeled the "suck-ups" and some good ideas never really got a chance to be tried and it took a long time before others were operational.

Systems theory is one of the more complicated frameworks for understanding organizational behavior and development. However, it may be the most important theory we have. It suggests that every unit (e.g., team) is a system within a larger system (e.g., organization). What goes on within the team affects the organization and what goes on in the organization affects the team. There are many pathways to the same end point and the ripple effects of any of the changes within any of the pathways are likely to affect at least the parts of the organization closest to the team or the person who starts the ripple. Teams need to keep managers and union officials informed and respond to the leadership of union officials and managers. Teams need the support of union officials and managers. Teams cannot afford to be short-sighted. Organizations cannot afford to allow teams to go off in any direction they please. Plans must be made interactively, and constructive external relations are necessary between and among all elements of a system if effective teams are to be built.

Relations with "suppliers" (i.e., any person or group that provides materials, tools, or work for a team) and "customers" (i.e., any person or group that receives anything that the team produces) are most important to teams. Teams also must look at their relationships with "competitors" (i.e., any person or group that could be doing some or all of the work that the team is doing now or could be doing in the future). Teams need a game plan for how to at least keep up with their competitors. Some questions that could serve as an agenda for a team meeting called to examine external relations are as follows:

- Who are the "customers" or "clients" of your team?
- Who are the "suppliers" of your team?
- Who are the "competitors" of your team?
- Which additional people or groups does your group have to deal with at least occasionally?
- How do people (individuals and groups) outside of our team describe the team?
- Which relationships should the team:
  Try to benefit more from?
  Try to improve on?
- Who will do what to/with whom by when in order to help the team with its external relations?

If it becomes clear that the team needs to develop a more comprehensive plan for improving its external relations, Lewin's force-field analysis framework should prove to be useful. The steps of Lewin's framework essentially guide the team through identifying its current state of external relations; what they think the relationships could/should look like; what forces exist that are pushing toward improving external relations; and what forces, barriers, and sources of resistance might interfere with improving external relations. The team would then pick which forces for and which forces against change deserve priority attention. The team develops plans to capitalize on the forces for improvement and reduce or eliminate the forces against change. Exercise 21 provides an outline for this activity, which is modeled after Lewin's framework.

EXERCISE 21

A Force-Field Analysis of Your Team's External Relations

Directions: Use a separate sheet of paper to chart your analysis of each step as described below.

Step 1. Analysis of the current situation

Describe the current state of your team's relationships with key nonteam members and groups. In doing so, try to consider: Which relationships are constructive now? Which relationships need to be improved? Overall, what are the strengths and weaknesses of the pattern of your team's external relations as they exist now?

Step 2. What is the preferred future situation

Describe what your team's external relationships would look like if they were truly constructive and mutually satisfying. What would they be like if relations were to become fully successful over the next one or two years?

Step 3. Forces for change

Identify each of the forces pushing for the changes that are needed to successfully achieve the "vision" you described in step 2. What existing forces might help close the gap between the situations described in steps 1 and 2? In responding to this question, consider: What do you think your team and organization has going for it that helps you believe that successful change is possible? What do you anticipate happening during the next year or two that will help establish changes in relationships with your team? What sources of support will push you and your team to establish more effective external relationships?

Step 4. Forces against change

Identify each of the forces that might hold back the changes needed for your team to develop truly constructive relationships. What forces exist that might interfere with closing the gap between the situations described in steps 1 and 2? In answering this question, consider: What obstacles, barriers, pitfalls, sources of resistance, and so on, do you believe might interfere with efforts to accomplish the vision described in step 2?

Step 5. Estimating the strength of the forces for and against

Estimate the strength of each of the forces listed in steps 3 and 4 by using a 1 to 10 scale in which a 1 rating represents a force

EXERCISE 21 continued

that should have almost no effect on efforts to move toward successful change and a 10 rating represents a force that could have a tremendous impact on change efforts. Use the ratings to identify the major forces for and against changes in your team's external relationships.

Step 6. Develop plans to deal with the forces

6A. Develop plans to capitalize on the top two or three forces for change. These plans will help you sell the changes needed to improve relations between your team and key individuals and groups external to your team. Spend some time developing these plans, but keep in mind that it is even more important to develop plans to reduce the forces against improving relations.

6B. Develop plans to reduce or eliminate the top two or three forces against change. Be sure the plans spell out strategies to overcome the obstacles, barriers, pitfalls, and sources of resistance that are (or could be) interfering with improving relations between your team and key individuals and groups external to your team.

Strategies for Dealing With Intergroup Conflict

Sports analogies are often used to discuss work team issues. However, keep in mind that the major goal of sports teams is to compete with other sports teams. If work teams compete with each other, the organization may suffer. I have often used a game called "Do As Well As You Can!" to raise the awareness of work teams to the potential negative consequences of competition. In this exercise, I divide the team or teams I am working with into four subteams and physically separate them in the room as much as possible. I tell them that they are the four key departments in my company and I need their independent advice each "marketing period" on whether to sell apples or oranges. The instructions for the game, which is a variation of the old "Prisoner's Dilemma," appear in exercise 22.

The game nearly always brings out the competitive nature of teams and a tabulation of the corporate bottom line shows how overall profits suffer as a result. Team representatives will often be able to

EXERCISE 22

Do As Well As You Can!

Directions: Your "team" will be asked to decide whether to sell "apples" or "oranges" each marketing period. The corporation keeps track of how well each team is doing. At the end of the year, the corporation would like to provide a bonus to those teams that do well. Follow the steps below to determine what your team will sell.

The payoff matrix for each marketing period is as follows:

- If all four teams sell apples, each team loses $1,000,000.
- If three teams sell apples and one sells oranges, the three sellers of apples gain $1,000,000 each and the one seller of oranges loses $3,000,000.
- If two teams sell apples and two teams sell oranges, the two sellers of apples gain $2,000,000 each and the two sellers of oranges lose $2,000,000 each.
- If one team sells apples and three teams sell oranges, the seller of apples gains $3,000,000 and the three sellers of oranges lose $1,000,000 each.
- If all four teams sell oranges, each team gains $1,000,000.

There will be seven rounds, or marketing periods. The payoffs (gains and losses) are tripled for round three and multiplied by 5 for round 5 and by 10 for round 7. Assume the teams are so far away from each other and so busy that they do not have time to consult with each other. *Decisions for each round must be made privately without any verbal or nonverbal interaction with any other team.* However, just before rounds 3 and 5, one representative from each team will meet in the hallway and discuss selling strategies for four minutes. The corporation is counting on your wise decisions and will reward those teams that do well. Please keep track of the payoffs as we go through this year together.

Marketing Period	Time Allowed	Payoff Formula	Current Profit/Loss Record
1	2 min.	Regular	_____
2	2 min.	Regular	_____
3	4 min. for reps	3 x Regular	_____
	2 min. for team		_____
4	2 min.	Regular	_____
5	4 min. for reps	5 x Regular	_____
	2 min. for team		_____
6	2 min.	Regular	_____
7	2 min.	10 x Regular	_____

gain a cooperation agreement during the meetings held just before periods three and five, but some group typically fails to follow through. The exercise is thus also useful for exploring trust issues and the need to communicate across teams.

Structural Approaches to Dealing With Intergroup Relations

Once the team is aware of the dangers of competition and has reviewed the current state of their relations with key players and teams, strategies for improvement need to be developed. One of the more basic approaches to dealing with intergroup issues is to establish policies and structures. These may be as simple as establishing a few decision-making rules or more complex strategies such as integrating whole departments. The strategy should depend on the degree to which the groups are interdependent and/or need to share information with each other. Sometimes it is nice to keep others informed but is not truly necessary to accomplishing tasks. Other times, neither group can be successful unless the work of each is closely coordinated. The following is a hierarchy of strategies based on the criteria of need for information flow and task interdependency:

- Integrating departments
- Permanent problem-solving committee
- Temporary task forces
- Liaison members assigned across groups
- Planning and resource allocations to reduce interdependency
- Appeal to hierarchy
- Rules and regulations
- Physical separation

At a very basic level, when two teams do not need to work with each other for task purposes and yet seem to engage in disruptive conflict, the organization may be able to separate the parties to avoid unnecessary conflict. If physical separation is not possible, it would help to establish clear rules and boundaries regarding making decisions that might affect the parties. Having no rules in this regard can set up a power vacuum and inadvertently encourage competitive behavior in the form of power struggles. Since all circumstances cannot be anticipated and you do not want a rule book that is thick and cumbersome, some conflicts should be resolved by simply having each party present their case to a manager in a higher-level position in the organization's hierarchy. This is not ideal if the parties need to have a great deal of contact with each other, but it will suffice if the interaction and interdependency needs are low.

Some conflict can be dealt with proactively through planning. If you can anticipate that problems will arise as work demands increase or procedures change, superordinate goals and strategies and implementation plans should be jointly established to clarify expectations and ease anticipated transitions. If the parties will need more information from each other in order to make plans for themselves, a liason/contact person can be assigned to and from each of the groups involved. These key linking pins would attend meetings of the other departments to share information and to ensure that their home departments are aware of issues going on in other departments that may eventually affect them.

As particular intergroup problems are identified, special task forces composed of representatives from the affected parties could be formed. These task forces would be expected to use a systematic problem-solving procedure such as the 4-A method and report their recommendations and implementation plans to the appropriate authority figures in the organization and, ultimately, to their home departments. While a task force would disband after making such recommendations, a permanent cross-group committee would continue to meet on a regular basis if the interaction/interdependency requirements are high. Ultimately, if the work of the parties is so intimately tied together, the departments may need to be merged. This restructuring strategy would necessitate a review of all of the Seven Key Components of Effective Teams to ensure that the new team is effective.

Resolving Other Intergroup Conflicts

Warner Burke (1975) offers a technique known as intergroup mirroring for situations in which the main cause of the conflict centers around a lack of understanding between the groups. After conducting interviews to verify that conflict is disrupting the functioning of the organization, a meeting is held on site that is chaired by a person (or persons) in the organizational hierarchy who is responsible for the teams involved. The responsible party explains that an off-site session will take place to investigate and, hopefully, resolve the differences between the parties and establish the ground rules for the meeting. In particular, there must be some clarity regarding what decision-making boundaries must be adhered to in the effort to resolve the disputes.

The off-site session is divided into three phases: Imaging, Sharing and Confronting, and Bonding. After a brief introduction to remind the groups of the purpose and ground rules for the session, the groups are sent to separate rooms to complete the Imaging phase. They are asked to answer three questions: (1) How do we perceive ourselves as a group? (2) How do we perceive the other group? and (3) What do we predict the other group will say about us? All answers are then recorded on flipcharts that are posted in a neutral room to begin the second phase (Sharing and Confronting) of this process. The groups are expected to read each other's answers but are not allowed to attack or defend the statements. Then the groups are asked to develop a list of all the discrepancies in perceptions that exist. For example, Group A may have described itself as ambitious, while Group B may have described Group A as vicious. It is very important that participants abide by all the ground rules and that the discussion emphasizes discovering differences, not attacking and defending. After a complete listing of the discrepancies is recorded, every individual has the opportunity to rank order the list according to which discrepancies are causing the biggest problems between the groups. These rank orderings can be averaged or, if time permits, the parties can be asked to reach a consensus decision regarding which few key discrepancies are causing most of the problems. In the final phase (Bonding), several cross-team task forces are formed to investigate the top discrepancies and develop recommendations regarding what should be done to reverse the damage these differences in perceptions have been causing. All the key parties, possibly including the key authority figures responsible for these teams, are brought together to listen to the recommendations and decide what actions will be taken. Table 18 summarizes the steps involved in the three phases of Burke's intergroup mirroring technique.

While I have found Burke's technique to be useful when two groups are in conflict, I have sometimes been confronted with situations in which several groups are not getting along. In one large plant, for example, we actually had eighteen different groups working at cross-purposes with each other. They said unpleasant things about each other, complained about who should be allowed to do which types of activities, and criticized even the progress made by

Table 18 The Intergroup Mirroring Technique

Phase 1: Imagery

■ Each group develops an image of itself and the other group to surface stereotypes, myths, untested assumptions, misperceptions, and the potential causes underlying the conflict. Each group is given a private room to brainstorm answers to the following questions:

What are we like as a group? (When answering this question, consider: What is our image of ourselves? What are our characteristics? What is it like to work in this group? What are we like to work with?)

What are they like as a group? (When answering this question, consider: What is our image of the other group? What are their characteristics? What is it like to work with them?)

What is the other group's image of us? (When answering this question, consider: What do we predict they will say about us when they answer question 2?)

Phase 2: Sharing and Confronting

■ Groups return to a common room and post their answers to the questions on flipcharts on the walls.

■ Groups read each others' answers and ask clarification questions only (e.g., "Help me understand what you mean when you state...as your perception of us or of yourselves").

■ Each group develops another list. This one identifies the discrepancies in perceptions between its own image and the image the other group has of it.

■ Groups share their lists of discrepancies and constructively confront the differences.

■ Together the groups generate another list that identifies the discrepancies that need to be worked out. The groups then prioritize the issues.

Phase 3: Bonding

■ Cross-group task forces are formed to address the priority issues. (Note that sometimes it is a good idea to provide some training in problem solving and/or conflict resolution before these task forces begin this assignment.)

■ Each cross-group task force is also asked to identify injustices each group has caused or experienced; what would motivate the groups to collaborate more in the future; the competencies/resources each group has to offer the other group; and the next steps that should be taken.

---

other groups. We rented the ballroom of a large hotel and arranged for eighteen other "break-out" rooms. The plant manager and the local union bargaining chair addressed the crowd and talked about the need for change. They emphasized that while these groups were fighting with each other, the business' competition was eating their lunch. They said that the day was to be dedicated to sharing feedback with each other and that plans to improve relations would have to be developed by the end of the day. I was asked to facilitate the process, which I call the "Post Office Technique." The intervention resulted in a significant reduction in dysfunctional conflict. Several groups established liaison members. Other pairs of groups formed joint task forces to plan and coordinate future activities. However, three groups continued to play "turf wars" with each other. After three months of allowing them to work this matter out on their own, the Steering Committee disbanded one of the groups and established clear rules regarding the interaction between the other two. The steps for using this process with teams at your location is provided in exercise 23.

Five Styles of Group Interaction

In chapter 8, five basic approaches to resolving interpersonal conflict were described. These styles—avoidance, accommodation, competition, compromise, and collaboration—have also been used by Thomas (1976) and others to analyze intergroup interaction. Interactions between groups can be examined according to the importance of each group's goals and the degree of compatibility among the goals. When the goals are incompatible and are not very important to either of the groups, then an avoidance strategy is appropriate. Separate the groups in some way such as giving them office space in different parts of the building. The groups should not be invited to the same meetings. These strategies could lead to the elimination of unnecessary conflict.

When the groups' goals are compatible but the goals for a given project are not deemed as particularly important, the accommodation strategy could be appropriate. Both groups should be allowed to proceed on their own. There is no strong need for investing time interacting other than to keep the relationship smooth. Requests for information should be accommodated, but limited energy or resources should be expended in working together.

When the goals of the two groups are incompatible and yet each group views its own goal as important, competition between the groups is likely to surface. A reexamination of the interests underlying the goals may help identify the basis for a collaboration. However, in a world of limited resources, there will be situations in which one group succeeding means that the chances of another

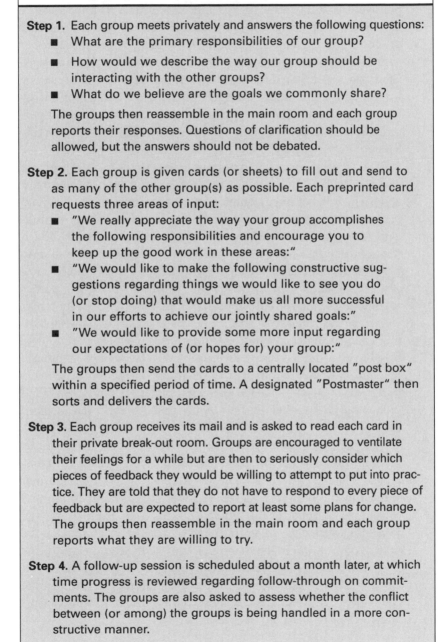

EXERCISE 23

The Post Office Technique
for Intergroup Conflict Resolution

Step 1. Each group meets privately and answers the following questions:

- What are the primary responsibilities of our group?

- How would we describe the way our group should be interacting with the other groups?

- What do we believe are the goals we commonly share?

The groups then reassemble in the main room and each group reports their responses. Questions of clarification should be allowed, but the answers should not be debated.

Step 2. Each group is given cards (or sheets) to fill out and send to as many of the other group(s) as possible. Each preprinted card requests three areas of input:

- "We really appreciate the way your group accomplishes the following responsibilities and encourage you to keep up the good work in these areas:"

- "We would like to make the following constructive suggestions regarding things we would like to see you do (or stop doing) that would make us all more successful in our efforts to achieve our jointly shared goals:"

- "We would like to provide some more input regarding our expectations of (or hopes for) your group:"

The groups then send the cards to a centrally located "post box" within a specified period of time. A designated "Postmaster" then sorts and delivers the cards.

Step 3. Each group receives its mail and is asked to read each card in their private break-out room. Groups are encouraged to ventilate their feelings for a while but are then to seriously consider which pieces of feedback they would be willing to attempt to put into practice. They are told that they do not have to respond to every piece of feedback but are expected to report at least some plans for change. The groups then reassemble in the main room and each group reports what they are willing to try.

Step 4. A follow-up session is scheduled about a month later, at which time progress is reviewed regarding follow-through on commitments. The groups are also asked to assess whether the conflict between (or among) the groups is being handled in a more constructive manner.

group succeeding are diminished. If that is the case, the key strategy is to ensure that it is a fair fight. Both groups need to feel that their points of view were taken seriously and both parties had an equal chance of "winning." Competition, up to a point, can produce the positive stress that encourages each team to deliver its full potential. However, if the playing field is not level or if either team is composed of "poor sports," bad feelings are likely to result. Those who lose get even, as was pointed out in chapter 8. Situations that call for competition can seriously reduce the long-term effectiveness of the use of teams in an organization. Competition generates dangerous energy in an organization. The energy must be channeled toward the superordinate goals of the organization or to a process that produces a collaborative approach.

When the goals are very important to the groups and the goals are also compatible, the situation is ideal for using the collaborative approach. Collaboration requires a lot of work, time, effort, skills, and patience. It can produce highly creative solutions to complex problems. It also promotes long-term constructive relationships. Although this approach may be ideal in many ways, it cannot be force fit onto every interaction between teams. Sometimes the goals are not compatible. Sometimes there isn't sufficient time to bring the parties together to use the win–win approach. Sometimes collaboration may violate federal regulations when it results in collusion between suppliers and customers. Despite these warnings, most teams should be urged to consider increasing their use of the collaborative approach. It is the most underutilized style of group interaction. Not many teams realize the potential for working together with individuals and groups outside of their turf. Potential gain for everyone involved exists.

The final type of intergroup interaction is called the compromise. It is appropriate when the goals are moderately important and compatible. The issues need to be dealt with but may not be important enough to use the more aggressive styles such as competition and collaboration. Splitting the difference helps each group feel it got something out of the interaction and didn't just accommodate the other group. However, if both groups know that a compromise is the likely result of an interaction, gamesmanship strategies such as a "high ball–low ball" approach often are utilized. This lessens the credibility of communications between the parties and reduces trust levels, as was pointed out in chapter 8.

Summary

Effective teams must establish diplomatic ties with key players and other groups in order to succeed within an organization. Changes within one team will affect others. Organizations need teams to work together for the common good. Each team should identify who its "suppliers," "customers," and "competitors" are. Each team should know how these people view them. Each team should develop strategic plans to build good constructive relationships with others. Lewin's force-field analysis provides a framework to develop these plans. Activities such as Exercise 22, "Do As Well As You Can!", build an awareness of the need to collaborate. Interventions such as intergroup mirroring and the post office technique were provided in this chapter to assist those teams experiencing conflict with other teams. Seven structural strategies for managing intergroup interactions were also provided. These strategies are to be used, depending on the level of interaction and interdependence required. Finally, it was recommended that if the goals of two teams are quite compatible, supportive interaction strategies such as collaboration and accommodation are best. If the goals are very incompatible, the strategies of competition and avoidance are better options. Compromise approaches are used when the levels of goal importance and compatibility are moderate. These strategies take into account the fact that teams need to develop strategies that help build ties with the people and groups external to their membership.

PART THREE

Evaluating and Maintaining Team Success

A few decades ago, it was still possible to see a sports team win the championship year after year. The New York Yankees and the Boston Celtics of the 1950s and 1960s, the Montreal Canadians of the 1950s, and the UCLA Bruins of the 1960s all had multiple championship seasons. In more recent times, if a team wins back-to-back titles or what is called a "three-peat," it is considered a monumental accomplishment. Times have changed. The rate of change has changed. Is it any wonder that it is difficult to sustain success with work teams year after year? In the last two chapters of this book, we will examine the many reasons why teams get stuck, how to evaluate where your teams are now, and provide some additional strategies for enhancing team effectiveness. Since no two teams or organizational settings are exactly alike, you will need to be able to react to a myriad of issues and problems that others won't even have to address. A troubleshooter's guide to a variety of these problems is provided in this section of the book to assist your efforts to help the teams in your organization.

The old cliché that "the only thing constant is change" certainly holds true for teams. If you are going to take teams seriously, you cannot rest on your laurels. The process of team building involves a repeated cycle of data-gathering activities; followed by a collaborative analysis of that data by the very people who provided it; followed by some action planning regarding what to do about the conclusions reached during the analysis; followed by still more action and a return to data gathering. Teams stay stuck when any point of this cycle is abandoned. Teams offer organizations many potential benefits, but they definitely require much upkeep. Never let someone "sell" you on the team concept with the idea that it will make your job easier. It will change the nature of all the jobs of those involved. It should make jobs more satisfying and meaningful, but it also requires effort. The team concept must be continually improved. It never becomes perfect. You have to keep up with things to make improvements.

Teams change people as well as organizations. The original vision you had for the team concept at your organization may have involved treating people with respect and seeking their input on matters relevant to the tasks that they perform. The people on those teams may come to expect this as a bare minimum standard of how employees should be treated. People may want to have decision-making power, not merely provide input. People may learn how connected their jobs are to the overall success of the organization and may want to influence decisions beyond the confines of their department or function. Teams evolve, and, if no plan accounts for this evolution, you may end up with a revolution; or, worse yet, you may end up with frustrated employees who now know that their capabilities for helping this organization are not being utilized. The team concept approach is actually a complex educational strategy aimed at improving skills, beliefs, structures, and processes. When the employees are educated en masse, leadership must be competent. Wise leaders know that they do not have to be smarter than everyone else. They just need to know how to organize all the intelligence available from all the teams.

Ideas must lead to actions. The challenge to organizations using the team concept is how to utilize the tremendous resources that knowledgeable human beings bring to a situation. It may actually be easier to start a team concept than it is to sustain it. Chapters 11 and 12 will provide you with the information and resources to address the challenge. The team concept vision, the plans for implementation, and the efforts to address each of the Seven Key Components of Effective Teams must be continually upgraded. Let's take a look now at one organization's efforts to do just that.

Case Study

Adjusting a Team Concept Across Time in a Large Unionized Firm

The plant was part of a chain that produced large, heavy-duty equipment. This was the biggest plant in the chain, with 3,500 employees at this location alone. Relations between the union and management had been adversarial at the national and the local levels for years. A particularly long and bitter strike led the parties to include a Letter of Agreement in their contract to allow any location to attempt to develop a team problem-solving process to improve quality, satisfaction, and labor relations. Only one of the eleven U.S. facilities even attempted to invoke this provision during the three years of the contract. However, the letter was reinstated in the next contract, and several facilities decided to explore the possibilities.

In this particular case, the local union leadership and management decided things couldn't get much worse, so they hired a consultant to hold an off-site meeting to see what could be done. For a day and a half, people yelled and swore and blamed each other for everything that had gone wrong over the last twenty to thirty years. None of the ten people present had less than fifteen years of seniority, and they all had vivid memories of past wrongs. Eventually, albeit reluctantly, they unanimously concluded that things had to change. They agreed to the consultant's request to gather data from a representative sample of people throughout the plant.

Surveys were administered to about 200 people and about 60 people were interviewed. The results were not surprising. People felt the relationship between the union and management was bad and hurt everyone. Morale was very low. People felt they had all kinds of ideas that could improve job satisfaction, the product, and the company's profits. However, people also felt that trust levels were so low that most people would not share the ideas that they had.

A joint Union–Management Steering Committee was formed. They attended training sessions on team building, problem solving, conflict resolution, and communication skills together. They visited the site of a well-known company that had successfully used some problem-solving teams. They agreed to appoint two full-time coordinators (one hourly and one salaried employee) to carry out a plan that included the launch of four departmental problem-solving teams and two cross-functional task forces. Membership on these teams was strictly voluntary. Management went out of its way to ensure that the recommendations of these early teams were implemented. Most of the ideas involved making work areas cleaner, safer, and more pleasant. The union leadership stood up to the challengers at meetings in which the opposition caucus accused them of selling out. Waves of four to six teams were launched every two to three months. Each team received thirty-two hours of training in the same topics the Steering Committee undertook. Some of the teams addressed scrap rate and other quality issues.

After about eighteen months, the Steering Committee asked the consultant to gather some more data. He used most of the same interview and survey questions, but sampled a larger number of people. The data were kept confidential but coded in order to analyze whether attitudes differed between those in the sample who had gotten involved and those who had not yet joined a team or task force. The difference was dramatic. The more involved a person was, the greater she or he reported being satisfied. The Steering Committee decided to adjust its plan for teams. It agreed to add six new full-time "facilitators" and increase the number of problem-solving teams to be launched over the next twelve months. It also decided that all managers and elected union officials (stewards, committee members, executive board members) were to receive training in participative leadership skills. They wanted the teams to push for change from the bottom up and the leadership style training to serve as a push for change from the top down. They also wanted teams to focus on problems that they believed would affect customers. Not all members of the Steering Committee were convinced that this was a good idea, but, ultimately, they agreed to rename their process the Customer and Employee Satisfaction Process (CESP).

The Steering Committee continued to meet on a fairly regular basis and relations between the key union and management leaders improved. At the same time, the grievance rate dropped over 85 percent. Teams were asked to make presentations at professional association conferences and to facilitate workshops at other plants in this company's chain. Subcommittees on communications and training were formed and reported each month to the

Steering Committee. During this year, teams came up with an additional $2 million in cost savings, beyond what it cost for the training and the meetings. Problems also arose. The waiting list for becoming a team grew to the point that it would take a person months from the time they volunteered to join a team to when they could be scheduled for training. Supervisors reported that some team members slept or read the paper during meetings and did not contribute ideas. Teams were upset by the length of time that it took for them to get approval for their ideas and the even longer time it took to get their ideas implemented. A union leader who was also a member of the Steering Committee was put on disciplinary leave and threatened to "pull the plug" on all CESP activities. The plant manager was transferred to another location and the son of a corporate vice president was named as the new CESP coordinator. It appeared that it was time to gather more data.

Surveys and interviews were again used and it was determined that expectations had accelerated. The Steering Committee developed a new strategic plan that established four Joint Implementation Teams to expedite responses to teams in the four areas of the plant. It was also decided to designate a portion of one area to experiment with self-directed work teams. This involved a huge investment in the facility itself. Machines were moved from all over the plant so that each designated team was producing a whole, identifiable product. The teams elected their own leader and were given more training and access to all production and cost records. Some of the teams were able to work out processes that allowed them to achieve production rates that exceeded expectations. Others never reached the break-even point. Efforts to improve in this area continue. The hope is that eventually the whole plant will consist of self-directed work teams.

Meanwhile, negotiations for the next labor contract have broken down at the national level. Support from the international union and from the corporation for team concept experiments is being drastically reduced. Support from the local union and management leadership continues, in part, because the members of the teams and committees won't let them back down. Every year brings new challenges. Every year they generate a new strategic plan for the use of teams. They are trying to get better every year, but the standards for such judgments change every year. They are taking teams seriously. Teams are seen as the vehicle for enhancing organizational effectiveness and employee satisfaction by local management and employees alike.

This case study shows the need for continual attention once the steps toward a team concept are taken. Data must be gathered and plans must be made. Most importantly, actions must be taken. The material in the next two chapters should give you some understanding of why your teams will stall; data you can gather in order to monitor their health; and strategies to address problems and help your teams evolve to their next level of excellence.

CHAPTER 11

Sustaining Team Success

L aunching and developing effective teams might seem difficult, but wait until you witness those teams getting stuck and experiencing difficulties. Team concept change efforts are not quick fixes for organizations. Team concept changes that are one-shot efforts at least require booster shots. More realistically, if you want a team concept change effort to be cost effective, you must be dedicated to making team building a continuous improvement effort. No team is ever perfect; there is always room for improvement. Your organization needs a long-term strategic plan that illustrates the role that teams will play for future success. Each team needs at least a twelve-month plan of the things it needs to do to sustain and advance its effectiveness and satisfaction levels.

Why Teams Get Stuck

All teams experience ups and downs. Why do many organizational development efforts fade away eighteen months or so after their implementation? There are at least as many reasons for this as there are letters in the alphabet. In fact, since so many popular change efforts are known by their acronyms (e.g., EI, QWL, TQM, SDWT), let's take a look at the problems that could derail a team concept change effort letter by letter. These problems are summarized below.

A Is for Allocation of Resources

Time, money, and people must be allocated to keep the change effort going. Sustaining team concept efforts may mean stretching these allocations too thin after the first wave of teams are launched. How many teams can your organization launch and nurture at any given point in time? After your teams have received their initial training and organizing meetings, do they get additional opportunities? If every team needs time to meet, when will there be time for production? Keep in mind that the team concept requires time and money.

B Is for Burnout

People get tired of meetings. The people who show enthusiasm at the launch of team concept efforts end up on too many committees, task forces, and so on. At first, it feels good to be able to express one's frustration over the way things are done around the organization. Now the responsibility to do something about the problems is on the team's shoulders. People get tired of tackling problem after problem. After a while, it feels like it takes twice as long to get half as much done. Then you know you are experiencing team burnout. After you have wall-to-wall teams, where are you going to find the new blood to reenergize your change effort?

C Is for Cycles

All relationships have cycles. No marriage or partnership works perfectly all the time. A natural characteristic of relationships is the need for renewal. Union–management relationships, which are at best shotgun marriages, also have cycles. Relationships between a group of employees and their respective managers are bound to experience dry spells.

D Is for Dudes

Team concept OD efforts often have too many dudes and not enough cowboys. As defined in chapter 2, dudes are people who can dress up like cowboys but can't ride horses. Many managers and union leaders have been able to dress up situations in the rhetoric of "teams," "participative management," "empowerment," "employee involvement," "win–win problem solving", "workplace democracy," and so on, but not very many have shown the capacity to ride these horses.

E Is for Exploiting Expectations

Publicity surrounding highly successful team concept efforts often makes it sound like it's mostly a matter of common sense. People may begin to believe teams will be the panacea to all their problems. Managers begin to expect no grievances. Workers expect to have decision-making authority over a large range of issues. And sometimes union leaders, key employees, and/or managers exploit these unrealistic expectations by using change efforts as a bargaining chip.

F Is for Fast Launches

Many team concept efforts have been launched too quickly, without adequate preparation for the people and/or the system. One-shot training sessions won't change years of habits. People need practice and a supportive system for change to stick. Managers, who are eager to show their bosses how many teams they have going, are prone to create this problem, which has led to the collapse of many team concept efforts.

G Is for Gamesmanship

Managers, workers, and union representatives know that organizational life includes some politics and games: "If corporate or international union leaders want this change, fine, we'll give it to them." Compliance to the wishes of the top can get you short-term success, but true commitment is needed for long-term success. Managers who view a team concept intervention as the latest fad to come down from corporate are most likely to play the "wait it out, but go through the motions" game.

H Is for the Hawthorne Effect

Some of the early success of any change effort can be attributed to what is known as the *Hawthorne Effect*. The idea that because it is new, because people are being paid attention to in some cases for the first time in a long time, some improvement in satisfaction and performance levels can be expected. However, once the uniqueness of a team concept effort wears off and you try to institutionalize the processes into the fabric of organizational life, you will not be able to count on Hawthorne Effects to achieve results.

I Is for Incompetence

Some managers, team members, and union representatives have been able to rise to their level of incompetence within their respective organizations (a.k.a. the Peter Principle). Effective teams require talented members, coaches, and owners. Team concept efforts cannot serve as long-term substitutes for competent management and leadership. Furthermore, managing and leading groups in a participative manner requires skills above and beyond those needed to perform such roles in the traditional manner. Not all managers and leaders will be good at practicing these new skills. Weak links can stall out a team concept effort.

J Is for Jaded

Most managers and employees have witnessed the failure of previous efforts to promote change in their organization. Many of them have felt they were burned by the risks they took. Many will be cynical and sarcastic about the long-term chances for success with any change effort. This jaded outlook is likely to surface when mistakes occur within the team concept process. Since no process has been or can be operationalized perfectly, mistakes are inevitable and the cynicism will be unleashed and will have to be addressed.

K Is for Key Champions Leaving

Facilitators and coordinators who have succeeded in helping a local plant or facility obtain positive results with a team concept have sometimes been promoted to corporate positions or have been chosen to work on the international union's staff. General managers who were true supporters of a change effort also move on to other career assignments. Efforts that are dependent on the enthusiasm and skills of a few key people are very vulnerable.

L Is for Luck

Bad luck strikes some OD efforts. Such factors as downturns in the economy, breakthroughs accomplished by competitors, and natural disasters create obstacles that must be overcome to sustain a change effort. Timing can't always be controlled.

M Is for Middle Management

The people in the middle of the hierarchy are all too often left out of the planning and benefits of a team concept effort. They are told and/or sold the ideas of the process by their bosses. They perceive what status and power they had to be eroded by the sharing of the decision-making process. They see top management and leadership and the rank-and-file benefiting, but they want to know what's in it for them. What about the quality of their working lives? Furthermore, they see the team concept as a threat to their job security as organizations move to flatten their hierarchies and push decision making to lower levels. Middle-level managers have subtly sabotaged more team concept efforts than perhaps any other group because of these perceptions; but can we blame them?

N Is for Needs

Team concept change efforts attempt to promote continual change and self-renewal, but many people have strong needs for stability. The stress generated by change and assessment creates excitement, but it also creates uncertainty. Some people live with uncertainty better than others. Some may block the effort because of their need for stability.

O Is for Obstructions Within the Process Itself

The paperwork, procedures, and bureaucracy created to manage and institutionalize team processes is a two-edged sword. Structure is needed to legitimize the process, establish standards, reduce redundancies, and ensure follow-through, but the myriad of committees and reports frustrate some promoters of change and add to the workload of many people.

P Is for Psychological Rewards

When you have never been asked to contribute your ideas on how to make your group's work life more effective and satisfying, you may be excited by the opportunity. The psychological rewards of involvement and of seeing your ideas put into action carry many team concept efforts for a year or two. However, participation processes will eventually generate feelings of inequity if workers perceive their efforts to benefit only the company, with "nothing in it" for the participants. Some concrete and visible incentives—even financial—are likely to be demanded after the initial nurturing period of a team concept launch. Never forget that reward systems are subject to negotiations by the proper authorities.

Q Is for Quick Solutions No Longer Available

During the initial launch of the change effort, many small problems can surface and be dealt with quickly. As time goes on, groups uncover deeper and more complex problems that often require cooperation across departmental lines. These larger issues take more time to address, and groups often feel frustrated and bogged down as discussions continue on and on without any visible signs of improvement.

R Is for Rationality That Dulls Emotional Charges

The philosophy and rhetoric of team concept ideals can stimulate exciting and emotional discussions. Once commitment to these concepts is established, however, the hard work of rationally developing solutions to workplace problems may be less exciting, at least to the people attracted to teams as a philosophical movement to change systems. We complain and gripe with righteous indignation about the lack of common sense underlying some organizational practices and decisions. However, the systematic application of common sense and rational problem-solving procedures requires discipline that may be difficult to get excited about.

S Is for Sacred Cows

Management, and the union, generally establish a list of issues that they feel should not be discussed in teams. Across time, groups may become less willing to accept these restrictions and may also come upon issues that management, or the union, wishes it would have placed on the sacred cow list originally. These threats to established powers may lessen their commitment, and/or the existence of these sacred cows may lessen the credibility of the participative process in the eyes of lower-level employees.

T Is for Turf Building and Protection

As groups identify their problems, they may attempt to solve them at the expense of other groups. Competition for resources can become a stumbling block, especially after the system has already launched many teams.

U Is for Upper Management and Union Leadership

Unless high-level leaders actually model participative leadership behaviors, their commitment to team processes will be questioned. Top-level leaders may be accused of saying that teams are good for lower levels of employees but fail to be team players themselves. Words *and* actions are needed. Employees will look for clear signals from the top on this issue.

V Is for Visibility Diminished

The first successful pilot team receives visibility. If you are the second or twentieth group to succeed, your accomplishments may be discounted with inferences that you were able to follow where number one led. If a later group fails, it's even worse. Couldn't they even copy successfully? Beyond this issue, it is just logistically difficult to provide unique recognition for groups when many groups exist within an organization.

W Is for Wrong Things Are Learned

Managers and leaders sometimes interpret training on participative styles to mean "let your people do it all." They attempt to learn to use a laissez-faire approach, rather than an active democratic approach. The lack of direction and modeling may result in groups wandering aimlessly. In addition, some groups, managers, and leaders seem to learn that participative decision making and rational problem solving are things that take place during team meetings, which take place once a week, rather than learn the processes that need to be incorporated into the daily business of work.

X Is for the Xerox™ Effect

When an initial team succeeds by using a particular technique or after benefiting from a particular training program, subsequent groups may attempt to make a "Xerox copy" of that technique or experience, rather than duplicate the process the earlier group used to generate a solution or strategy that uniquely addresses its problems.

Y Is for Yardsticks

Many team efforts fail to establish the yardsticks that will be used to help measure success and failure. While it's admirable to allow such processes to evolve, frustrations occur when people don't know what is expected of them. It is also difficult to diagnose and correct why a team concept effort has stalled, when it was never certain where it was supposed to be headed. Of course, improperly chosen yardsticks that are rigidly applied will also create major problems. Team concepts led by a human resources staff that is uncomfortable with measurement issues will be seen as soft and nonbusiness related.

Z Is for Zombie Effects

Zombies, according to legend, are people the spirit world won't allow to die. Some teams, groups, task forces, and even entire OD processes should be allowed to die. The "magic" that worked elsewhere won't work everywhere. Pushing too hard and too long on a system or group of people may produce long-term damage. Readiness for change is a key requirement for success with the team concept.

Evaluating Where You Are in the Process

Whether you feel your teams are stuck or not, you should periodically evaluate their current level of effectiveness and satisfaction. This will provide you with the awareness of the need for change and/or give you another opportunity to celebrate progress. Exercise 24 provides a simple activity to help get teams started on efforts to evaluate where they are in the team cycle.

EXERCISE 24

What Day Is It in the Life of This Team?

Directions: Each team member should respond to the questions below. Each member can then share his or her responses with the entire team.

1. When you look back on the history of this team, what do you believe are the highlights of its existence?

2. What do you believe are the lowest moments in the life of this team?

3. Based on your review of the historical data, what would you ask your teammates to pay particular attention to?

4. Based on your review of the historical data, what element could you most positively influence?

5. What is your personal peak moment as a member of this team?

Six Key Factors to Evaluating Teams

If you decide to encourage your organization to attempt a serious and systematic review of its progress with its team concept efforts, there are six key evaluations that should be performed.

Goals

Is the team concept accomplishing its prescribed goals? This should also be evaluated on a team-by-team basis. Chapter 4 emphasized that each team must have a set of measurable goals that serve as targets for the team. The data for this analysis should be available to the team on a daily basis, if at all possible. Thus, evaluation is actually an ongoing responsibility of the team and the organizational systems must be prepared to provide the team with the relevant information it needs.

Reactions

How are people reacting to the team concept? How satisfied are members with their team? To what extent are people who are external to most teams feeling positive about what the teams are doing for the sake of the organization? Is the team concept helping or hindering morale? Has customer satisfaction improved since the advent of teams? While "hard data" such as productivity levels, absenteeism, and customer complaints should be examined, people's perceptions/ reactions will always be important to assess as well. If they do not perceive the team concept to be in the best interests of employees and the company, the change effort is likely to fail.

Learnings

How has the team concept expanded people's knowledge and skills? Has the investment of training and the opportunities to get involved resulted in people being able to do things better? Are the human resources of the organization now more valuable as a result of the team activities? What can people do and what do they know now compared to the time before there was a team concept at your organization? The team concept should be assessed along these lines because it is really a complex educational strategy for organizational change.

Cost/Benefits

Has the team concept been worthwhile? What costs have been accrued due to your efforts to establish a team concept? How much has train-ing cost? What is the dollar value of the time being spent in meetings? Have any investments in physical facilities been made to accommo-date the team concept? What benefits have been accrued due to your efforts to establish a team concept? Have cost-saving ideas been gen-erated? Have absenteeism, grievance, and turnover rates reduced in those departments in your company where the team concept has been implemented? What are the dollar values associated with these reductions? Has the quantity or quality of production improved? It is likely that you will be able to document the costs more easily than the benefits. You may not be able to fully credit the team concept for some improvements. However, if you compare improvement rates in areas where teams exist versus areas where you have yet to launch teams, you should get a pretty good idea of the cost–benefit ratio of your efforts. Since any change effort takes some time to get used to, you will need to give teams time to work together before estimating any improvements. Although you will be dealing with numbers, remember that evaluation of any organizational development effort is more of an art than a science.

Process

Has the process you have used to launch teams been effective and efficient enough? Is the structure you have established (e.g., Steering Committee, Design Team) provided a clear sense of organization and a communication channel? Are teams being launched too quickly? Not quickly enough? Is the training developing the knowledge and skills team members need? Is the organization being responsive enough? Are resources, including facilitation help, being provided? Are the rules for teams appropriate and clearly understood? Have upper management and union leadership continued to demonstrate their support for the team concept? What else could they be doing? The results of the team concept effort may be assessed through the previous four categories, but this category asks you to look at how the concept was operationalized. This assessment can help you improve your efforts to launch teams in other parts of your company.

The Seven Key Components of Effective Teams

Have the teams gotten better or worse on each of the Seven Key Components of Effective Teams? The *Team Diagnostic Questionnaire* (TDQ), or whatever survey or interview questions you used prior to launch, should be administered regularly. If the scores on the items of the TDQ are lower after the team concept has been in place for three to six months, it may be that members have higher expectations now that they have become involved. You may need to add the phrase, "Compared to the last time you evaluated your team..." before each of the items on the TDQ. However, if scores on any items remain consistently low or significantly decrease, you might try one or more of the strategies suggested below or any of the exercises suggested in chapters 4 through 10 to enhance team effectiveness:

- Find a few significant projects or goals that would cause people to work together as a team. Choose one or more of them to work on this year. (Hint: Be sure that people are contributing their own area of expertise when working on these projects.)
- Adjust the mix of players on the team (e.g., add or delete from the membership of the team, add temporary resource people on an ad hoc basis, restructure the team into two or more teams) to enhance the talent component or provide more training.

- Develop a strong coleadership strategy (e.g., someone more externally oriented and someone more internally oriented, someone more task oriented and someone more relationship oriented; split up the roles of chairperson, facilitator, recorder; someone from a product line plus someone from service and a general manager) to enhance effectiveness.
- Agree to certain set procedures for meetings, problem solving, planning, and decision making. Make sure your team actually uses these procedures on a systematic basis and then teach the same procedures to other teams in the organization.
- Build greater loyalty to this team by spending more time together building closer, more trustful relations (e.g., social get-togethers, dedicated agenda time to relationship building exercises; convene a retreat).
- Establish a recognition and/or reward system that reinforces team-oriented behaviors. Incorporate the system in your communications with the organization and in your performance review system. However, remember that any organization-wide compensation system must be negotiated.
- Constructively use external pressures to get this team to pull together (e.g., present information to managers and staff together, make a collective presentation to the board or at a conference, publish an article about your team's team-building efforts).

Using Evaluation Data as a Basis for Strategic Planning

Table 7 in chapter 4 described the five steps of strategic planning—reviewing, assessing, problem solving, futuring, and action planning. Developing a strategic plan for enhancing team effectiveness is something that should be done on at least an annual basis. Organizations that are taking teams seriously will demand this. The planning process and the changes agreed to through that process should go a long way toward sustaining any effort to utilize a team concept. The evaluation data and review exercise described on the previous few pages will help your team accomplish steps one and two of this plan, reviewing and assessing.

Step three suggests applying a systematic problem-solving model such as the 4-A method described in chapter 7 to the issue of team effectiveness. Thus, the team is expected to brainstorm the many problems making it difficult for the team to sustain success. The team is then to analyze the chief causes of the major issues prohibiting success. The team generates the many and innovative alternatives the team might consider to eliminate or reduce these causes. Finally, after picking the best among the imperfect alternatives, the team pinpoints who will do which actions with whom and by when in order to implement the alternative. Instead of reserving the problem-solving procedure for production problems alone, this shows that the model can help the team help itself grow and develop. It also renews the discipline agreed to by the team.

Sustaining a team concept often requires more than fixing the current problems the team is facing. It often requires an expansion of the vision of the team concept. The Steering Committee needs to be prepared to reexamine the boundaries it originally set for the teams. The futuring step of the strategic planning process involves identifying new elements not originally planned for. If the original plan called for teams to work as employee involvement problem-solving teams once a week and report their recommendations to the Steering Committee, perhaps it is time to expand this to a self-directed work team concept. The scope of problems and responsibilities handled by the teams must expand across time. The authority to actually make decisions as opposed to recommendations should also be considered. The rewards available to teams may also have to expand across time. Praise and recognition may reinforce early efforts to be team oriented but, as was pointed out in chapter 9, monetary rewards really tell what is valued in business organizations.

Changes in the scope of issues, the level of authority, and the opportunity for financial rewards can help sustain a team concept effort but will also renew fears of the concept as well. Just when the Steering Committee may have thought its work was complete because so many teams have been launched, it must realize that a process requires ongoing planning efforts. Again the authority figures on the Steering Committee must make sure that the promises of changes are actually delivered. A detailed action plan developed in conjunction with the teams that are working to "get unstuck" should be published and monitored. While love may mean "never having to say you are sorry," taking teams seriously means "always saying what you are going to do and then doing it." This demonstrates commitment. This shows that teams are a genuine business strategy, not just a passing fad. This develops the trust needed to sustain success with a team concept.

Summary

There are many reasons why it is difficult to sustain success with a team concept. Commitment to gather evaluation data on an ongoing basis will help determine when teams are getting stuck. Systematic use of the Seven Key Components of Effective Teams and the strategic planning and problem-solving procedures described in previous chapters will help get teams unstuck. In sports, we sing high praise of those few teams that are able to repeat their success as champions season after season. Our work teams must also undergo a renewal process to repeat as champions as well. The problems teams face will vary from organization to organization. This chapter provided processes to use to deal with these problems. The next chapter will attempt to anticipate questions you may have regarding specific aspects of team concept efforts and some suggestions regarding what to do about those issues.

CHAPTER 12

A Troubleshooter's Guide to Creating Team Excellence

The previous chapters provided readers with the concepts and strategies to prepare for, launch, and sustain efforts to utilize a team concept as a serious business strategy. However, each organization has unique circumstances that will require adjustments in efforts to establish effective and satisfying teams. This chapter will provide answers to some problems and concerns you may still have. It concludes with the core features of the approach to teams advocated by this book.

How Does the Team Concept Differ in New Plants Versus Already Existing Facilities?

If it has been decided to institute a team concept at a brand new facility, the selection of employees should include an investigation of how skilled each person will be at working with others in groups. Past behavior is the best predictor of future behavior. Interviews about previous experiences with teams should be supplemented with group simulation exercises. This is time consuming and thus likely to be costly. However, it should save you some costs associated with training, since, at the very least, you will be selecting people very capable of learning team concept skills. Having made working in teams a condition of employment, performance appraisal, discipline, and reward systems that reflect team orientations will be easier to institute.

Introducing teams in a new facility will also mean having less "collective baggage" to deal with. There will not be a history and a culture that contradicts the values underlying the team approach that many existing facilities have to cope with. However, you also will not have the experience, knowledge of personnel, and comfort levels many existing organizations already have. The team concept can work in both environments, but implementing it in an already-existing facility means you need to honor the lessons you have learned from your history, both positive and negative. You may need to help people let go of parts of the past and focus on current realities and future demands. In both cases, a key to success will be having a sound business reason for the use of teams.

What Role Does the Union Play in a Team Concept?

In a unionized firm, the elected leadership must be treated as an equal partner in any team concept efforts. It is in management's best interest to involve the union at the very beginning of any such efforts. Management should resist drafting a vision statement or a plan and only asking the union to react (i.e., accept or reject) to it. This may get you compliance, but it won't get you commitment. Joint development of a team concept from the very beginning produces ownership. Both parties should be educated in the team concept together. If the two parties do not start out with the same information, how can they be expected to arrive at the same conclusions? Communication of team concept vision statements and plans often has more credibility when union leadership makes the announcement. If management said the same thing, it might be perceived as selling and be resisted more readily.

It may take a little longer to get started in a joint setting, but the likelihood of a longer-term success story is increased. This is, in part, because the two parties can keep each other honest about the promises they make to employees. It would also take two parties to back away from the team concept once it got started. The literature is full of many reports of unions (most notably, the United Auto Workers and the United Steelworkers) who have supported experimentation with teams. In fact, Wellins, Byham, and Wilson's (1991) study of executives reports lack of management support to be a bigger problem than lack of union support. There are some splinter groups and certain key local and national union leaders who do not support experimentation with team concept ideas. These officials typically either suspect that the purpose of the team concept is to reduce the number of jobs or they fear that support of a joint activities process like teams will make them look like they are cozying up to management and will cost them their positions in the next election. Expect unions to push for greater employment security provisions in exchange for support on team concept issues, as well they should. Remember, the union has the legal responsibility to negotiate changes in wages, hours, and working conditions, so do not have teams negotiating these provisions. Work with the union leadership, and together the experiments with team concept ideas may grow into all kinds of successful organizational development interventions.

Do You Need a Consultant to Launch a Team Concept?

It depends on whether you have an internal person to champion the cause who also has the time, credibility, and expertise necessary to succeed. Sometimes a consultant will only say what you already know, but the organizational members need to hear it from an outside source. It is an old joke that a consultant is any ordinary person more than fifty miles away from home. Any consultant that you might use must be value-added. However, beware of consultants who are willing to do all the work for you. A consultant should be able to help save you the time and energy needed to reinvent the wheel, but you and other members must fully own the process. Ownership comes from creating something. Beware of consultants who have a canned program for teams. At the very least, these programs need to be modified to fit your situations and employees. Beware also of consultants who specialize in team building. While they may have the experience that can be useful to you, they may see a need for team building wherever they look. The consultant should know more things about teams and organizational change efforts to be worth his or her charges, but no outsider will know more about your company than key insiders within the organization. A partnership between the external and internal change agents will serve you and your organization best.

What If a Given Individual
Just Refuses to Be a Team Player?

Many people do not like to depend on others when it comes down to their livelihood. A few others have personal problems or have failed to develop the interpersonal skills needed to work effectively with others. They may not want to become a member of a team. They may not want to work with a particular group of people. Most individuals who are difficult to get along with have a good reason for their behavior. They feel they were treated very unfairly at some point in their career, and they probably were. We need to help these individuals vent their feelings one more time and then invite them to let go of the past. This can be very difficult.

You are probably not there to serve as a counselor to such people. In the world of work, we need to assume that everyone is an adult and should be treated as an adult. Adults are given choices and are expected to live with their decisions. At some point, you need to either confront these difficult people (see chapter 8) or give them some choices and live with their decision. The choices might include choosing the group they wish to become a member of, joining a team, leaving the company, or attending training sessions developing the skills needed to work effectively with others on a team. If the person was hired without any expectation that she or he was supposed to work with others, perhaps the individual could be given an assignment with limited interaction with others, if the tasks to be accomplished allow for such an arrangement. I know an organization that did this. All nonteam-oriented employees were placed on individualized jobs within the same location of their plant. The area became known as the leper colony.

How Do You Deal With Middle-Level Managers
Who Sabotage Team-Building Efforts?

Whenever there is resistance to change, the first step is to discover the nature of the resistance. The sources of resistance will likely be lack of understanding, lack of ownership, fear of loss of status or control, and fear of job loss. Upper management must have some private conversations with middle managers. The rationale, vision, and plan for teams must be clearly explained. Emphasize the business reasons for instituting the team concept. If you have failed to have middle-management representation on the Steering Committee or Design

Team, you should at least seek their input on how the plans should be modified to increase the likelihood of their success. Devise other structures to keep middle management informed and involved. Be sure you find ways to make use of input that would make things better.

Clarify your long-term commitment to the team concept and support your words with actions. Upper management must model the leadership style they want middle management to use. Training in the skills associated with that style should be offered. Teams of middle-level mangers should be formed and given significant assignments, for example, strategic planning and solving problems cutting across departments or across levels. Performance appraisals and reward systems must provide feedback on behavior that is helping or hindering the team concept. Most team concepts seem to lead to a reduction in the number of managers and levels in the hierarchy. Some have advocated making these cuts quickly and deep and then dedicating energy to orienting the survivors. Others provide job security promises to managers mirroring promises made to hourly employees. Offers of enhanced early retirement packages are made. Outplacement services are provided by others. Some companies give special (though isolated) assignments to managers who just don't seem to change to styles that nurture teams. There is no one answer to this issue. The best approach is to choose the strategy or two that best fits your company. Management's treatment of management is a key to long-term success with teams.

How Many Hours of Team Training Should We Provide Each Team?

I'm afraid this question misses the point of training. You provide training to enhance knowledge and/or skills. The number of hours needed for training depends on how many skill and knowledge bases must be developed, and this will obviously vary from team to team. As was pointed out in chapter 3, it is crucial to conduct a needs assessment before providing training. It is tempting to succumb to the convenience of scheduling everyone for the same amount of training, and it is tempting to play things politically safe by providing everyone with the exact same training. However, it is not cost effective and treats team members as if their experiences have not taught them anything about teams. Team training sessions should be organized by the objectives they are designed to accomplish.

Should You Start With Relationship Building Or Task-Oriented Skills When Preparing Teams?

This is a yin and yang issue. There are negative and positive aspects within each approach. If the team has serious relationship issues, it may be too painful or dangerous to confront them directly. The group may need to work on a task first and experience the ability to successfully work together. On the other hand, a group may never get around to learning how to do a task until it deals with the interfering relationship issues. The key thing to remember is that every team-building effort must emphasize the need for task and relationship skills. Some exercises are designed to deal with both at the same time but at different levels. For example, the icebreaker exercise described in chapter 8 has members practicing the three key relationship-building skills—sharing information, listening effectively, and providing constructive feedback—while discussing what their experience has taught them about working together on teams. You can modify the issues you want team members to share their experience about to focus on any task skill that has been identified as appropriate subject matter for team training.

How Far Should You Go With the Team Concept? Do Teams Really Call All the Shots?

Management must always manage. Union leadership must always fulfill its duty of fair representation. Team concept efforts influence the style in which these responsibilities are fulfilled, but they are never abdicated. In many ways a team concept turns the organizational hierarchy upside down, but this is probably best accomplished through evolution, not revolution. Teams represent a bottom-up strategy for organizational change. However, a top-down strategy of a change in leadership style must happen simultaneously. Since the early 1980s, the United Auto Workers and Ford Motor Company have emphasized that the movements toward employee involvement (EI) teams and participative management (PM) leadership style are two sides of the same coin that lead to continuous improvement.

Unless you are starting a new facility or have already extensively utilized different types of teams at your existing facility, you might want to develop a long-term phasing in process of a team concept. First, provide people the opportunity to volunteer for problem-solving committees within their existing work units. Later, form cross-functional task forces to address broader issues. Then begin to institute self-directed work teams. As was discussed in chapter 11, the scope and power of teams must grow across time. Committees, task forces, and self-directed work teams should probably be launched in waves of two to four at a time. This allows you to focus your resources to nurture each "crop." When teams are launched one at a time, they are often subject to the abuse of members of other departments. They are either accused of cozying up to management or they are resented for privileges—real or imaginary. Members of successful launches should be recruited on a temporary basis to be trainers and facilitators for the next wave of teams. It is often suggested that the ideal team size is six to twelve members. However, this really varies, depending on the scope of work the team is to accomplish, how routine the work is that is fulfilled by the members, and how much outside help the team will need. You should expect that it will take two to five years to fully institute self-directed work teams across a facility. This, of course, will also vary, depending on the number of employees, the teams, and the nature of the production or service process.

Do All Team Decisions Have to Be Consensus Decisions?

Consensus decision-making procedures, as described in chapter 7, lead to high-quality solutions to problems and greater commitment to making them work. However, they do take time and patience, and these qualities might be in limited supply. The bottom line when it comes to team decision making is that all team members must have a voice but no "bad mouthing" of the decision is to occur after it is made. There must be follow-through on all agreements associated with the decision or trust will erode. Some teams I have worked with adopted a rule that they will always attempt to reach a consensus. However, if no consensus can be reached after three attempts on a given issue, the team votes and if any option receives 80 percent of the votes, all team members will fully support that decision.

Should You Abandon All Individual Reward Systems?

Actually, rewards and recognition must be offered to individuals and to teams in order to build an effective team. Individuals need feedback in order to become more effective in their efforts to be team players. Chapter 9 provided a long list of possible means to offer the recognition needed. I would like to offer a word of warning, however, about giving "most valuable player" awards. Such awards encourage a competitive attitude toward fellow teammates. Reward individuals and teams for their abilities to surpass goals, standards, and targets. Provide recognition for individuals and teams for acting in a team-oriented fashion.

What New Jobs and Job Titles Have Been Produced Since Teams Have Become So Popular in Business Organizations?

Companies have been eager to provide clear indications that the organization has changed as a result of the movement toward self-directed work teams. Symbolic actions such as allowing each team to paint or redecorate their work space, alter or eliminate uniforms, dress casually, and do away with the wearing of neckties has become policy at some locations. Changes in the titles of jobs have also been instituted. If the change in job title is merely symbolic, one must question the sincerity of the effort. However, it probably is appropriate to change some job titles to emphasize the transformation of responsibilities that has taken place. First-line supervisors are now referred to as coaches, facilitators, advisers, or team consultants at various locations. Hourly employees are called associates, technicians, or individual contributors at others. New positions have also been established. Some hourly employees have been named or elected to be team leaders or team coordinators. If these individuals become nothing more than hourly supervisors, not much change has really taken place. If the hourly team leaders are truly players/coaches who work with people rather than control most decisions, then real change has taken place. Human resource departments have added job titles such as employee resource coordinators and team coordinators whose jobs consist of sitting in on team meetings, providing process observations, carrying out the policies of the Steering Committee, providing training, and monitoring implementation efforts. In unionized firms, these positions may be filled by hourly and salaried individuals who form a joint activities staff, enabling the team concept to generate its own internal career path for some.

What's Next for the Team Concept in Business Organizations?

It appears safe to say that the use of teams in business organizations is here to stay. It is just a matter of which type of teams will be emphasized, the range of decisions teams will be asked to address, and the degree to which the teams will be provided full authority to actually make the decisions. The use of self-directed work teams will remain the hot trend into the next century. As these teams become increasingly more prevalent and effective, an emphasis on involvement of teams in the strategic planning process of businesses is likely to increase. Business schools have begun to prepare managers of the future with team-building skills. Selection procedures for larger organizations have included more emphasis on the ability to work with and for teams. Smaller organizations have encouraged the "we're all in this together" philosophy for years. The need for employees to be flexible and work well with others is clear. Team skills will be crucial to most people's ability to hold a job in the twenty-first century.

The impact of the team concept on business processes is likely to be even more evident. Open-book management, gainsharing, flexible reward systems, and organic organizational structures are likely to be more common practices. However, the opportunity to work at home and network with others via computer information systems may either reduce an emphasis on teams or force us to expand our thinking about how to improve relations between team members who rarely meet face to face.

How Do You Know Whether You Are Ready for Teams? How Do You Know When You Have Made It?

Chapter 2 provided you with the questions to consider when preparing your organization for the advent of teams. However, you will never be perfectly ready for teams. If you want your organization to become more successful, it means you are considering change. In order for changes to take place, risks must be taken. Risks, by their very nature, require that you will sometimes succeed and sometimes fail. However, there is a difference between risk taking and gambling. In risk taking, you know there is a likelihood of some failure but there is a calculative notion that there is a good chance that success can occur. Gambling is a shot in the dark. You are ready for teams when you are a risk taker, not a gambler.

You will also never really "make it." That is, you will never perfectly achieve the vision of your team concept. Team development is a process, not a program. You have made it when measurable data show you that you are significantly better off than you were before. The problem with an anecdotal approach to evaluating your success with teams is that at any given point in time you will be able to point to things that are not going so well in addition to some testimonies of success.

Are you cursed with the plague of perfectionism? Do you use your analytical skills to point out the flaws of ideas and verify that things could or should be better? I hope you learn to celebrate significant improvement rather than hope for the impossible dream of perfection. I also hope that you keep your feet to the fire to push for continual improvement with your efforts to utilize a team concept. There are no perfect systems when it comes to human behavior. The goals should be to understand and come up with an approach that improves a situation and one's life. You will never have a perfect system for teams in your organization. However, if you seriously look at your situation and systematically apply the principles of teams addressed in this book, you will be able to significantly improve your organization's effectiveness and the satisfaction levels of the people on your teams. It is a matter of taking teams seriously and having realistic expectations.

Summary

This chapter addressed a series of issues that you may face in your team concept efforts. This book has attempted to systematically describe what is needed for building effective teams. Some key points to remember include:

■ The use of teams in business organizations is increasing for good reasons. However, you should never launch teams just for the sake of having teams.

- There are many types of teams in business organizations.
- Team development is a process, not a program.
- Effective and satisfying teams have seven key components:
  Clear sense of direction
  Talented members
  Clear and enticing responsibilities
  Reasonable and efficient operating procedures
  Constructive interpersonal relationships
  Active reinforcement systems
  Constructive external relationships
- Successful team-building efforts and successful leadership share the same two orientations of being simultaneously task- and relationship-oriented.
- The core task orientation skills are planning and problem solving.
- The five steps to successful planning are reviewing, assessing, problem solving, futuring, and action planning.
- The four steps to successful problem solving are awareness, analysis, alternatives, and action.
- The core relationship skills are communication and conflict resolution.
- Effective communications require sharing information in an interesting manner, listening effectively, and providing constructive feedback.
- There are five basic approaches to resolving conflict: avoiding, accommodating, competing, compromising, and collaborating.
- Every team gets into slumps; the key to getting unstuck is to renew relationships and utilize systematic planning and problem-solving skills.
- There is a systematic way to build effective teams. Do not attempt to utilize a team concept unless you are willing to take teams seriously!

References and Resources

Bachner, C., and M. T. Bentley. "Participation and Productivity: The Quality Circle Experience." In *Quality of Work Life: Perspectives for Business and the Public Sector.* Reading, Mass.: Addison-Wesley, 1983.

Bixenstine, V. E., H. M. Polash, and K. V. Wilson. "Effects of Level of Cooperative Choice of the Other Player on Choices in a Prisoner's Dilemma Game." Parts I and 2. *The Journal of Abnormal and Social Psychology* 66(1963): 308–313; 67(1963): 139–147.

Blake, R. R., and J. S. Mouton. *The Managerial Grid.* Houston: Gulf, 1964.

Blake, R., H. Shepard and J. Mouton. *Managing Intergroup Conflict in Industry.* Houston: Gulf, 1954.

Burke, W. W. "Managing Conflict Between Groups." In *New Technologies in Organization Development:* 2d ed. J. D. Adams, San Diego, Calif.: Organizational Associates, 1975.

Camp, R. R., P. N. Blanchard, and G. E. Huszczo. *Toward a More Organizationally Effective Training Strategy and Practice.* Englewood Cliffs, N. J.: Prentice-Hall, 1986.

Cavanaugh, G. F., D. J. Moberg, and M. Velasquez. "The Ethics of Organizational Politics." *Academy of Management Review* (July 1981): 363–374.

Cole, R. E. "Made in Japan-Quality Control Circles." *Across the Board* 16 (November 1980): 72–78.

Cole, R. E. *Work, Mobility and Participation.* Berkeley, Calif.: University of California Press, 1979.

Costin, H. *Readings in Total Quality Management.* New York: Dryden Press, 1994.

Dayal, I., and J. M. Thomas. "Operation KPE: Developing a New Organization." *The Journal of Applied Behavioral Science* 4, no. 4 (1968): 473–505.

Doyle, M., and D. Strauss. *How to Make Meetings Work.* New York: Jove Books, 1976.

Dubrin, A. *Contemporary Applied Management.* Plano, Tex.: Business Publications, 1982.

Ebbinghaus, H., as reported by G. Murphy and J. Kovach in *Historical Introduction to Modern Psychology.* New York: Harcourt Brace Jovanovich, 1972.

Fisher, R., and S. Brown. *Getting Together: Building a Relationship That Gets to Yes.* Boston: Houghton-Mifflin, 1988.

Fisher, R., and W. Ury. *Getting to Yes: Negotiating Agreeement Without Giving In.* Boston: Houghton-Mifflin, 1981.

Fleishman, E., E. F. Harris, and H. E. Burtt. *Leadership and Supervision in Industry.* Columbus, Ohio: Bureau of Educational Research, Ohio State University, 1955.

French, W. L., and R. W. Hollmann. "Management by Objectives: The Team Approach." *California Management Review* 17, no. 3 (Spring 1975): 13–22.

Frost, C. F., J. H. Wakeley, and R. A. Ruh. *The Scanlon Plan for Organization Development: Identity, Participation, and Equity.* East Lansing: Michigan State University Press, 1974.

Garfield, C. *Peak Performers: The New Heroes of American Business.* New York: William Morrow, 1986.

Goodman, P. *Assessing Organizational Change: The Rushton Quality of Work Experiment.* New York: Wiley, 1979.

Graham-Moore, B. E., and T. L. Ross. *Productivity Gainsharing.* Englewood Cliffs, N. J.: Prentice-Hall, 1983.

Hackman, J. R., and G. Oldham. "Motivation Through the Design of Work: Test of a Theory." *Organizational Behavior and Human Performance* 16 (1976): 250–279.

Hersey, P., and K. H. Blanchard. *Management of Organizational Behavior: Utilizing Humam Resources.* Englewood Cliffs, N.J.: Prentice-Hall, 1977.

Hirsh, S. K. *Using the Myers-Briggs Type Indicator in Organizations.* Palo Alto, Calif.: Consulting Psychologists Press, 1985.

Hirsh, S. K. *MBTI Team Building Program: Leader's Resource Guide.* Palo Alto, Calif.: Consulting Psychologists Press, 1992.

Hirsh, S. K., and J. M. Kummerow. *Introduction to Type in Organizational Settings.* Palo Alto, Calif.: Consulting Psychologists Press, 1990.

Huszczo, G. E. "Training for Team Building." *Training and Development* (February 1990): 37–43.

Huszczo, G. E. "The Long-Term Prospects for Joint Union-Management Worker Participation Processes." *Workplace Topics* 2, no. 2 (1991): 13–35.

Huszczo, G. E., and D. T. Hoyer, "Factors Involved in Constructive Union-Management Relationship." *Human Relations* 47, no. 7 (1994): 847–866.

Jung, C. G. "Psychological Types." In *Collected Works.* Vol. 6. Translated by R. F. C. Hull. Princeton, N.J.: Princeton University Press, 1971.

Katz, D., and R. L. Kahn. *The Social Psychology of Organizations.* New York: Wiley, 1978.

Katzenbach, J. R., and D. K. Smith. *The Wisdom of Teams.* Boston: Harvard Business School Press, 1993.

Keidel, R. *Game Plans.* New York: E. P. Dutton, 1985.

Keirsey, D., and M. Bates. *Please Understand Me: Character and Temperament Types.* Del Mar, Calif.: Prometheus Nemesis Books, 1978.

Kouzes, J. M., and B. Z. Posner. *The Leadership Challenge.* San Francisco: Jossey-Bass, 1990.

Latham, G. P., and J. J. Baldes. "The Practical Significance of Locke's Theory of Goal Setting." *Journal of Applied Psychology* 60 (1975): 187–191.

Latham, G. P., and K. N. Wexley. *Increasing Productivity Through Performance Appraisal.* Reading, Mass.: Addison-Wesley, 1981.

Lawrence, G. D. *People Types and Tiger Stripes.* Gainesville, Fla.: Center for Applications of Psychological Types, 1982.

Leavitt, H. J. "Suppose We Took Groups Seriously." In *Man and Work in Society,* ed. E. L. Cass and F. G Zimmer. New York: Van Nostrand, 1975.

Levinson, H., and S. Rosenthal. *CEO: Corporate Leaderhip in Action.* New York: Basic Books, 1984.

Lewin, K. *Field Theory in Social Science.* New York: Harper and Row, 1951.

Likert, R. *New Patterns of Management.* New York: McGraw-Hill, 1961.

Locke, E. A., and G. P. Latham. *A Theory of Goal Setting and Task Performance.* Englewood Cliffs, N.J.: Prentice-Hall, 1990.

Machiavelli, N. *The Prince.* Oxford University Press.

Macy, B. A., and P. H. Mirvis. "A Methodology for Assessment of Quality of Work Life and Organizational Effectiveness in Behavioral-Economic Terms." *Administrative Science Quarterly* 21 (1976): 212–226.

Mayo, E. *The Human Problems of Industrial Civilization.* New York: Macmillan, 1933.

McClelland, D. C. *Power: The Inner Experience.* New York: Irvington, 1975.

McCormick, E. J. *Job Analysis.* New York: AMACOM, 1979.

Mintzberg, H. "The Manager's Job: Folklore and Fact." *Harvard Business Review* 53, no. 4 (1975): 49–61.

Moorhead, G., and R. W. Griffin. *Organizational Behavior: Managing People and Organizations.* Boston: Houghton-Mifflin, 1992.

Myers, I. B., *Introduction to Type.* 5th ed. Palo Alto, Calif.: Consulting Psychologists Press, 1993.

Myers, I. B., and M. H. McCaulley. *Manual: A Guide to the Development and Use of the Myers-Briggs Type Indicator.* Palo Alto, Calif.: Consulting Psychologists Press, 1985.

Myers, I. B., with P. B. Myers. *Gifts Differing.* Palo Alto, Calif.: Davies-Black Publishing, 1980, 1995.

New York Stock Exchange. *People and Productivity.* New York, 1982.

Nora, J. J. *One Way.* Plymouth, Mich.: Plymouth Proclamation Press, 1990.

Nora, J. J., C. R. Rogers, and R. J. Stramy. *Transforming the Work Place.* Princeton, N.J.: Princeton Research Press, 1986.

O'Leary-Kelly, A. M., J. J. Martocchio, and D. D. Frink. "A Review of the Influence of Group Goals on Group Performance." *Academy of Management Journal* 37, no. 5 (1994): 1285–1301.

Pearce, J., and K. Ravlin. "The Design and Activation of Self-Regulating Work Groups." *Human Relations* 40, no. 11 (1987): 751–782.

Peter, L. J., and R. Hull. *The Peter Principle.* New York: Bantam Books, 1977.

Price, K. H. "Decision Responsibility, Task Responsibility, Identifiability, and Social Loafing." *Organizational Behavior and Human Decision Processes* 40 (1987): 330–345.

Riley, P. *The Winner Within.* New York: G. P. Putnam's Sons, 1993.

Senge, P. *The Fifth Discipline.* New York: Doubleday, 1990.

Shaw, M. E. *Group Dynamics: The Psychology of Small Group Behavior.* New York: McGraw-Hill, 1981.

Skinner, B. F. *Science and Human Behavior.* New York: Macmillan, 1953.

Stack, J. *The Great Game of Business.* New York: Doubleday, 1992.

Steiner, I. D. *Group Processes and Productivity.* New York: Academic Press, 1972.

Taylor, F. W. *Scientific Management.* New York: Harper, 1911.

Thomas, K. "Conflict and Conflict Management." In *Handbook of Industrial and Organizational Psychology,* edited by M. Dunnette. Chicago: Rand McNally, 1976.

Thomas, K. W., and R. H. Kilmann. *Thomas-Kilmann Conflict Mode Instrument.* Tuxedo, N. Y.: Xicom, 1974.

Townsend, R. *Up the Organization.* New York: Alfred A. Knopf, 1970.

Tubbs, S. L. "Team Leadership: A Systems Approach." *The Journal of Leadership Studies,* 1, no. 2 (1994): 28–45.

Tuckman, B. W., and M. A. C. Jensen. "Stages of Small-Group Development Revisited." *Group and Organization Studies* 2, no. 4 (1977): 419–427.

Von Oech, R. *A Whack on the Side of the Head.* New York: Warner Books, 1983.

Vroom, V. H. *Work and Motivation.* New York: Wiley, 1964.

Weber, M. *The Theory of Social and Economic Organization.* Translated by A. M. Henderson and Talcott Parsons. New York: Free Press, 1947.

Wellins, R. S., W. C. Byham, and J. M. Wilson. *Empowered Teams.* San Francisco: Jossey-Bass, 1991.

Zander, A. "The Origins and Consequences of Group Goals." In *Retrospections on Social Psychology* edited by L. Festinger. New York: Oxford University Press, 1980.

Index